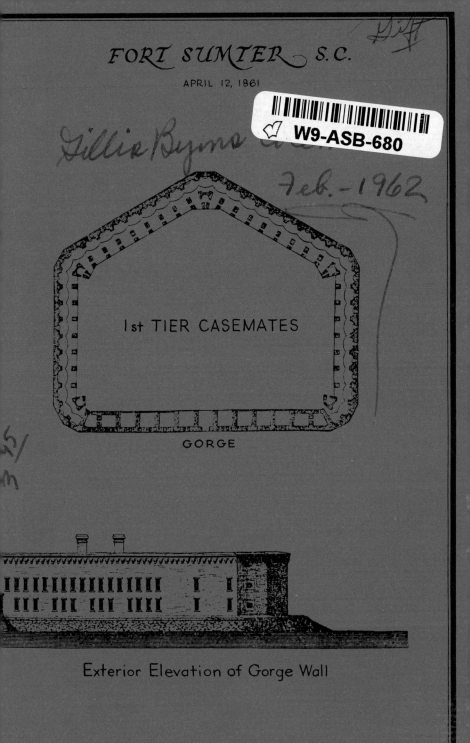

FORT SUMTER S.C.

APRIL 12, 1861

1st TIER CASEMATES

GORGE

Exterior Elevation of Gorge Wall

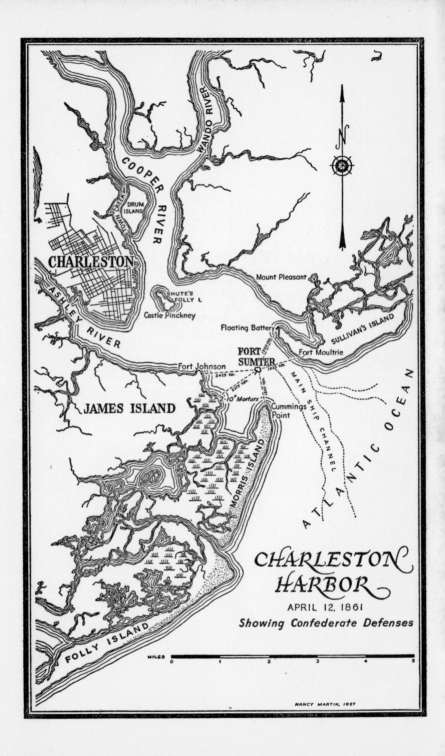

CHARLESTON HARBOR

APRIL 12, 1861

Showing Confederate Defenses

NANCY MARTIN, 1957

STORM OVER SUMTER

The Opening
Engagement of the
Civil War

by
Roy Meredith

Simon and Schuster
New York
1957

TO BOBBY

CONTENTS

"After four long, long years of war"

Edwin McMasters Stanton, Abraham Lincoln's energetic but humorless Secretary of War, sat at his cluttered desk in the War Department within hearing of the clicking of the military telegraph in the next room. He stroked his perfumed beard and almost smiled; he had reason to be pleased. It was Monday, March 27, 1865. The war for the Union was nearing the end of its fourth year, the South was clearly beaten, and the worst of the strain was over. He took up his pen and began to write.

GENERAL ORDER NO. 27:
At the hour of noon on the 14th day of April, 1865, Brevet Major General Robert Anderson will raise and plant upon the ruins of Fort Sumter, in Charleston Harbor, the same United States flag that floated over the battlements of that fort during the rebel assault, and which was lowered

by him, and the small force of his command, when
the works were evacuated on the 14th day of
April, 1861.

The ceremony at Fort Sumter would be a brilliant
occasion now that victory for the Union was assured.
It would also be a diversion from the serious work of
what appeared to be the last campaign. The flag, when
raised at Sumter, would be saluted by a hundred guns
and by a national salute from every fort and rebel
battery that had fired on Fort Sumter. Stanton hoped
that Major General William T. Sherman, whose recent
military operations had forced the surrender of
Charleston, would preside over the elaborate ceremonies.

Mr. Stanton put down his pen. Sumter had been
quite a beginning, he thought, a symbol of the North's
troubled unity from the start. As Attorney General in
President Buchanan's Cabinet, when the Government
had been wracked by conflict and indecision, Stanton had
sat across the table from Secretary of War John B.
Floyd, the Secessionist conspirator, and heard him urge
the withdrawal of Federal troops from the cluster of
forts in Charleston Harbor. In scathing denunciation
of Floyd's suggestion, Stanton had declared that any and
all who took a hand in the surrender of Fort Sumter,
the most potent base in the harbor, "would be commit-
ting a crime equal to treason and should be hanged."
As Lincoln's War Secretary, Stanton had inherited
from Floyd and the incompetent Simon Cameron an
indescribably chaotic department, but with crisis-driven
energy and a ruthlessness that bordered on dictator-
ship he had organized it into a smoothly running war
machine.

Stanton was now equally thorough in planning the ceremony at Sumter. Among the dignitaries he invited to participate were the Reverend Henry Ward Beecher, who would deliver the principal oration; Admiral John A. Dahlgren, Commander of the Atlantic Squadron; William Lloyd Garrison, the veteran Abolitionist; Adjutant General John A. Dix; Captain Gustavus Vasa Fox, Assistant Secretary of the Navy; and John George Nicolay, the Presidential private secretary, who would represent Lincoln.

In a letter to the Honorable Simeon Draper, Collector of the Port of New York, Stanton ordered that Draper permit such vessels as he deemed proper "to go to Hilton Head, to witness ceremonies at Fort Sumter, and carry as selected passengers such persons as you think may properly go," subject to all the military regulations of General Quincy A. Gilmore of Charleston. The Secretary telegraphed his plan to Mr. Lincoln, who was at City Point, headquarters of the Army of the Potomac, with Grant and Sherman, discussing the final campaigns of the war.

Lincoln was agreeable to the plan for the flag-raising at Sumter, but had one suggestion. "I feel quite confident," Lincoln wired Stanton, "that Sumter fell on the 13th, and not the 14th of April, as you have it. It fell on Saturday, the 13th; the first call for troops on our part was got up on Sunday, the 14th, and given date and issued on Monday, the 15th. Look up the old almanac and other data and see if I am not right." Stanton obediently made the change of date; but Lincoln's memory was strangely in error, and the date Stanton first proposed was subsequently adopted.

To his country, Major General Robert Anderson, the central figure in the ceremonies, was "Bob Anderson, my beau," the first Union hero of the Civil War. But in the embattled years that followed, his gallant stand at Fort Sumter had been nearly forgotten. Since October of 1863, while the titanic battles of Stone's River, Chickamauga and Chancellorsville were fought, while other soldiers were making great reputations, he had been retired from active duty for reasons of failing health. Robert Anderson was a fifty-six-year-old major when he fought his battle at Sumter. Shortly thereafter he was promoted to brigadier general and sent to his native state of Kentucky to assist in organizing and directing the Union forces there. Later, when in command of the Department of the Cumberland, he discovered the first symptoms of an illness for which there was no cure, an illness probably hastened in its progress by the prolonged mental and physical strain he had undergone at Fort Sumter: an Army medical report diagnosed it as "softening of the brain."

He had now reached the age of sixty, white-haired and feeble. Since coming to his New York home at 32 Fifth Avenue, on the corner of Ninth Street, he had spent most of his time taking solitary walks about the city, wearing a long, dark-blue military cape which hid his general's stars. When Sherman's invasion of Georgia and the Carolinas regained Fort Sumter for the Union, Anderson fondly recalled to friends he would meet in his walks that Sherman was once a cadet in his artillery class at West Point. "He is one of my boys," he said proudly, but he never talked about the high point of his own career of forty years of soldiering. Now Robert Anderson was to be honored in a ceremony at the fort he had defended so courageously.

On Sunday morning, April 2, the Reverend Henry Ward Beecher, after services at his church in Brooklyn, announced to his congregation from the pulpit that the excursion to Fort Sumter would take place on April 10 and that a limited number of tickets were available at the editorial office of *The Union*. The same day in Richmond, Jefferson Davis, attending church services in the family pew at St. Paul's, seated alone and erect, listening to the sermon of Mr. Minnegerode, was handed a dispatch from a mud-spattered Confederate officer. It read: "I advise that all preparation be made for leaving Richmond tonight. I will advise later, according to circumstances." The dispatch was signed "Lee." The President of the Confederacy quietly got up and left the church. That night Richmond fell to Union forces and the rampages of fire. The Confederacy was dead.

In New York, the demand for tickets for the excursion to Fort Sumter all but swamped the little office of *The Union,* and it was necessary to increase the passenger quota from one hundred and fifty to one hundred and eighty. Edward Cary, editor of *The Union,* arranged with G. S. Howland, president of the Neptune Steamship Company, for the charter of the steamer *Oceanus*. The sum of $18,000 was to cover passage and fare for the nine-day round trip, beginning April 10 and ending on April 19; each day over the time limit would cost an additional $2,500.

The passengers formed the "Sumter Club," elected Edwin R. Yale and Cyrus P. Smith president and vice-president, and drew up an "autographical" list of members which was given to the New York and Brooklyn newspapers. The Sumter Club, it ran, "extemporized in origin, unexampled in occasion; abounding with representatives of pulpit, press, forum and counting-room; graced with feminine beauty and culture; a synonym of patriotic devotion, would celebrate with feast of reason, and flow of loyal soul," the ceremonies at Fort Sumter. By April 8, all preparations were completed and the *Oceanus,* chartered by a portion of Mr. Beecher's congregation, had permission to clear for Charleston and Fort Sumter.

On Monday morning, April 10, the Fulton ferryboat, *Peconic,* largest of the East River ferryboats, left her slip at the foot of Montague Street, Brooklyn, to transfer the members of the Sumter Club to the *Oceanus,* moored at the Robinson Street wharf in Manhattan. Twenty minutes later the *Peconic* landed her passengers, and at ten minutes past noon lines were cast off and the *Oceanus* headed out into midstream to the playing of "Victory at Last" and the cheers of the crowds gathered on the wharf.

Aboard the steamer the passengers in holiday spirit filled every available space, shouted and waved hats and handkerchiefs until the ship was far downstream. The sky was overcast and before long a fine, filtering mist slightly dampened their ardor. Soon the rain increased and the fog began to thicken over the water. Governor's Island, Fort Lafayette, the heights of Staten Island and the sandy wastes of Coney Island were soon far behind.

Nearing Sandy Hook, the ship struck a sandbar. Captain Young raced the engines at full speed, but instead of moving, the vessel only churned the shallow waters into foam. Young hailed a passing steam tug, which came alongside and commenced pulling and hauling but without success. Soon a pilot boat came bearing down to within fifty yards and dropped a rowboat astern containing a pilot and two oarsmen. When the pilot came aboard, noting that the ship was aground at the stern, he ordered all the men to the forward deck in order to raise the stern. This caused some joking, but the "weight of corporeal and mental ballast," said Edwin R. Yale, "had the proper effect" and the *Oceanus* swung clear. Meanwhile the weather got worse and a heavy rain set in. One querulous committee member asked the pilot if they were still leaving that afternoon.

"You gentlemen want to go to Charleston, don't you?" the pilot asked. "Waal, you better lay here to-night, for its goin' to be a werry dirty, nasty night outside."

After a conference with Captain Young a vote was taken to decide whether to stay at Sandy Hook for the night or chance the storm. The majority voted to stay until morning. The anchor was dropped and the passengers spent the better part of the evening in the main saloon celebrating the news of Lee's surrender at Appomattox. By dawn the next morning the *Oceanus* resumed her course and headed south down the coast. "The hitherto staid steamer began to lose its reputatation for steadiness," wrote Edwin R. Yale, "and certain passengers, whose temperance and sobriety is proverbial, began to exhibit strange symptoms of inebriety." But aside from seasickness and the effect of a night's celebration of the end of a long and tragic war, the trip was enjoyable.

Good Friday, April 14, dawned bright and clear. A light shower during the night had brought a cool freshness to the air, and as the *Oceanus,* with the first morning light, crossed the bar and tied up at the Charleston wharf, members of the Sumter Club were standing at the rail. Breakfast was served at six o'clock and it was announced that the transports for

Fort Sumter would leave at ten o'clock. Before that time the passengers had time to assemble on deck to have their photograph taken and to stroll about Charleston, some of them returning with their arms filled with flowers.

Three and a third miles out in the harbor, Fort Sumter, or what was left of it, was gay with flags and bunting. On both sides of the main channel sleek steam frigates, stubby, double-ender gunboats, iron-clads, side-wheelers and double-turreted monitors of Admiral John Adolphus Dahlgren's Atlantic Squadron, each flying flags and pennants from stern to bowsprit, their guns loaded, lay at anchor awaiting the signal to take part in the ceremonies.

Inside, the fort looked like a huge earthwork, for as its walls had progressively been demolished during the war, the shattered brick and sand had fallen down in a slanting grade toward the center—a condition that had actually strengthened rather than weakened the fort. Surmounting the parapet facing Charleston were six large guns ready to fire a salute. As the members of the Sumter Club left the transport they climbed the fifty steps to the parapet, passed under an arbor entrance of evergreens and walked across thirty feet of earth and sand to the interior ruins of the fort.

In the center of the rubble-strewn parade, circular terraces of grass, marked off by immense conical shot and shell planted in the sand with their points upward, surrounded the new flagstaff. Before the flagstaff was a large platform carpeted with myrtle, mock orange, and evergreen, the railings festooned with boughs entwined with red, white and blue ribbon. Four pillars fifteen feet high, decorated with orange wreaths and the national colors, rose from the corners of the platform into graceful arches. At the very apex of the main arch stood a golden eagle. Rows of wooden benches were placed in a large semicircle to accommodate the five thousand guests, the rearmost center row with its back to the chimney of the old hot shot furnace.

As the huge crowd gathered they were disposed and managed by Colonel Stuart L. Woodford, who took charge of the exercises. While awaiting the arrival of Mr. Beecher and his party, the steamship *Planter,* her flag and walking-beam visible above the fort's parapet, slowly edged her way toward the wharf, followed a few moments later by the steamers *Arago* and *Delaware,* all from New York, whose passengers crossed the parapet and descended the stairway to the parade.

On the platform the main figures exchanged greetings. General Anderson, who had traveled from New York on the U. S. Military Railroad, wore a new blue uniform and military cape. Still handsome, though visibly aging, he took his seat next to his former chaplain, the Reverend Mathias Harris. It was now near noon and the ceremonies were about to begin. A hush fell over the crowd as Anderson slowly walked from the platform to the terrace and uncovered his head before the flagstaff. William Bradbury, the musical director, took his place at the head of the band and lead the audience in singing "Victory at Last." Then followed the familiar "Rally Round the Flag." Mathias Harris, who had read prayers at the first flag raising at Fort Sumter after Major Anderson had boldly moved his command there in December of 1860, stepped to the front of the platform.

Harris opened the ceremonies with a prayer and in a trembling voice pronounced a blessing upon the flag. When the old chaplain had retired to his seat, Brevet

Brigadier General E. D. Townsend stepped forward and read Anderson's official report of April 18, 1861, recounting the fall of Fort Sumter. General Townsend then read Secretary Stanton's order authorizing the ceremonies now taking place. At its conclusion, Sergeant Peter Hart, the old soldier who had seen service with Anderson as first sergeant in Mexico and who had volunteered for service at Fort Sumter, walked to the flagstaff carrying a new mail sack containing the original shot-torn flag which Anderson had lowered in surrender four years before. Saluting smartly, the old sergeant removed the flag from the mail pouch. At the sight of it the crowd burst into cheers. Three crewmen of the *Juniata* stepped forward and made the flag fast to the halyards with a wreath of evergreens, roses and mock-orange blossoms. Intense emotion showing on his handsome face, General Anderson stood in soldierly erectness, his white hair stirred by the breeze blowing across the parade. To those close to him he seemed to be living over again his terrible ordeal.

As he gazed at the broken fortress he once commanded, his eyes took in the shapeless pile of shattered walls, the mounds of rubbish and debris which still held the dank smell of powder and smoke, noted the dead images of dismounted guns half buried, their splintered carriages protruding from the rubble of bricks, timbers and mortar. Surveying this havoc wreaked by the guns of the Federal fleet, he probably recalled the herculean labors he and his men had exerted to mount some of the same guns. The fortress he had defended was, like himself, old, broken and shattered by the terrible events that began when a Southern shell from the mortar battery on Mount Pleasant burst over the parade, signaling the start of the struggle which had ended only a few days before.

After a long pause, General Anderson began to speak:

"I am here, my friends, my fellow citizens, and fellow soldiers, to perform an act of duty to my country dear to my heart, and which all of you will appreciate and feel. Had I observed the wishes of my heart, it should have been done in silence; but in accordance with the request of the honorable Secretary of War, I make a few remarks, as by his order, after four long, long years of war, I restore to its proper place this flag which floated here during peace, before the first act of this cruel Rebellion." Taking the halyards in his hands, he continued. "I thank God that I have lived to see this day, and to be here to perform this, perhaps the last act of my life, of duty to my country."

As the sound of his closing sentence drifted over the crowd he hauled the flag to the top, where, as if by a signal, the breeze blowing in from the sea unfurled it. The guns of the fleet opened with a shattering salute, followed by the firing of a hundred guns from batteries mounted atop the parapet. Sumter's big guns thundered and roared, and the sand stirred up by the recoil from the blasts was driven into the eyes of the audience. The victory cannonade lasted for a half hour, after which the audience, dusting off their coats, composed and reseated themselves to listen to the next grand exercise.

When the echo of the last gun rolled across the sky a round of cheers greeted the Reverend Mr. Beecher as he came forward on the platform. Edwin R. Yale ob-

served that Beecher seemed quite impressed with himself, aware that he was speaking quasi-officially and that
everything he said "would be regarded, not only as the
voice of the authorities at the Capital . . . but would
pass from that hour into history." Four years before
the minister had been burned in effigy in Charleston; his
fiery speeches against slavery had inflamed the hatred
of the Southerners and contributed to speeding the outbreak of the war.

Removing his gray felt hat, he shuffled the thin papers of his manuscript. For a moment his composure
was ruffled as a strong northwesterly wind almost blew
them away. Holding the papers firmly in both hands,
he began to read:

"On this solemn and joyful day, we again lift to
the breeze our father's flag, now, again, the banner of
the *United States,* with the fervent prayer that God
would crown it with honor, protect it from treason,
and send it down to our children, with all the blessings
of civilization, liberty and religion. Terrible in battle,
may it be beneficent in peace."

Halfway through his long oration he had to pause to
rest his voice while the band again played "Victory at
Last." Mr. Beecher continued:

"We offer to the President of the United States our
solemn congratulations that God has sustained his life
and health under the unparalleled burdens and suffer-
ings of four bloody years, and permitted him to behold
this auspicious occasion of that national unity for
which he has waited with so much patience and forti-
tude, and for which he has labored with such disinter-
ested wisdom."

The ceremonies ended with a final burst of applause
and cheers while every battery in the harbor which had

fired on Fort Sumter roared in salute. The band struck
up yet again "Victory at Last" and the audience
joined in the chorus:

"Our flag is free; we'll nail it to the mast.
Yes, we'll nail it to the mast, boys, nail it to the mast,
For there's victory, victory at last!"

The ceremony was over. The crowd dispersed to
their transports for the return to Charleston. General
Anderson, accompanied by Mr. Beecher, General
Townsend and other dignitaries, made his way slowly
up the stairs to the parapet. When he reached the top
of the stairs, he turned and looked back at the deso-
late, forlorn ruin of the fort for the last time. A few
small groups of citizens still lingered about the flagstaff.
Behind the last row of benches, on a mound of debris
that was once the forge of Fort Sumter, a photographer aimed his camera for one last picture of the parade and empty benches.

That evening, at a theater performance in Washington, the actor John Wilkes Booth fatally wounded the
President of the United States, Abraham Lincoln.

CHAPTER ONE | Prologue to Conflict

On its elegant and teeming surface, Charleston, South Carolina, in 1860, flourished proud and opulent. Her people fanned an essence of luxury and refinement and abetted a spirit of pageantry. The epitome of antebellum urbanity, Charleston also nurtured elements of discontent and disruption.

A population of 29,000 whites and 37,000 slave Negroes lived together in apparent harmony and mutual reliance. Together they managed, by tacit agreement and established practice, to keep their city, the largest south of Baltimore, a bastion of charm, energy and firm tradition.

Charleston's buildings dripped with jasmine and myrtle; her streets were wide and handsome and bore exotic names like Kimlock's Tower, Longitude Lane, and Horlbeck's Alley. The predominantly red brick and white marble architecture was softened by clusters of cypress and magnolia blossoms and Spanish moss hanging in delicate tassels from the trees.

All day the most important streets were jammed and noisy with draymen's carts and wagons and elegant imported coaches jostling for space. Down near the harbor, at the lower end of town, were the Battery and Esplanade and the fashionable churches, St. Michael's and St. Philip's, and the Bond Street theater—all meeting places of the rich whose coachmen were expert in getting them there on time. Young Negro boys leaned daily over the wooden guardrail and threw their baited hooks into the blue waters which were soon to churn with falling shells and carry the echoes of massive batteries.

This city of astonishing beauty and grace embraced a mode of living that would fade forever within a few years. Charleston men hunted and gambled, imported horses and lace, vases and livery from the great cities of England, France and Italy, and sent their sons abroad to be educated. Charleston ladies dressed themselves in foreign stuffs and sparkled at banquet and ball.

The courtly and Continental manners of prewar Charlestonians were often carried to extremes. As late as 1851 medieval tourneys tore up the lawns of the best plantations. Duels were still frequently fought, right up to the war, under the auspices of a club formed for that romantic purpose. These two forms of diversion, at once civilized and barbaric, reflected the cultivated and moneyed leisure that permeated Charleston's upper crust, too vigorous for decadence, too wealthy for plain hard work.

The Duc de La Rochefoucauld, after a visit to South Carolina, wrote, "From the hour of four in the afternoon the people of Charleston rarely think of anything but pleasure." With afternoons given over to pleasure, Charlestonians still managed to keep themselves one of the highly cultured segments of American society. It was not unusual to find among them a man who could enjoy Lucretius, Horace, and Sophocles in the original or to see the poems of a Charleston resident, Henry Timrod, known as the "trumpet of the Confederacy," in the journals of the day. William Gilmore Simms, hailed by Edgar Allan Poe as "immeasurably the best writer of fiction in America," was a distinguished author and a Charleston citizen. John C. Calhoun, the South's most eloquent spokesman, was also a native.

Cultural Charleston was enhanced, too, some years before the war, by the arrival of what came to be known as the "Codfish Aristocracy." This group was made up of Bostonians with whom the South had traded cotton, a South Carolina staple, and who had found Charleston to be such an agreeable city that they had moved and settled there. Their coming prompted a friendly cultural rivalry with their opposite numbers in the Charleston aristocracy.

Charleston was not isolated in any way, supporting many parts and peoples. The city was first settled in 1670. It figured in the War of Independence by twice withstanding British attacks, then surrendering to the armies of Sir Henry Clinton and Lord Cornwallis, who held on to it until 1782. In 1783 Charleston was formally incorporated as a city. Two holocaustal fires, one in 1795 and the second in 1800, nearly destroyed her, but her people rebuilt Charleston each time and made her even more lovely.

Although at different times the flags of Spain and

France had flown over the city, Charleston was essentially English in tone and manner and flourished so brilliantly that her crops of rice, cotton, corn and indigo made her the leading agricultural city of the old South and the principal market for six neighboring states.

Charleston enjoyed a prosperity agreeable in any age. Business boomed, imports and exports achieved a record high. The recently completed Charleston and Savannah Railroad had doubled commercial activity; banks and loan companies blossomed healthily. Building contractors were kept busy, and three colleges, eleven fire departments, a new water supply system, two gas companies, and forty-five manufacturing establishments within the city limits answered Charleston's needs. Bricklayers, carpenters and ordinary laborers generally received higher wages in Charleston than they did in Pittsburgh, Chicago, or Lowell, Massachusetts—and they also paid out less for rooms and board.

But Charleston's wealth could not be reckoned in products and culture alone. It was her labor which swelled her value. By 1806, 21,189 Negro slaves lived and worked in South Carolina, and their number increased. In the agricultural economy of the South, slaves were absolutely essential; they sometimes brought as much as $2,000 apiece when sold at market. Realizing that his whole economic structure depended on slave labor, the Southerner was dedicated to preserving it—even at the price of disassociating himself from the Union. One of the reasons most operative in the Secession movement was the fear that "foreign" agents would cause a slave uprising. Congressman Lawrence M. Keitt wrote privately: "Our

Negroes are being enlisted in politics with poison and fire. How can we stand it? I confess this feature alarms me." Because South Carolina was so wealthy, the people of Charleston were especially and emotionally involved in guarding what they deemed their rights.

As early as 1832, their leader, Calhoun, persuaded the State Legislature of South Carolina to declare the Federal Tariff Acts of 1828 and 1832 null and void and to take an extreme states' rights stand against them. The acts, he felt, were prejudicial to the agricultural South and favored the industrial North. In a strong statement, Calhoun proposed that if the Government of the United States should attempt to enforce the acts, the state of South Carolina would proceed forthwith "to organize a separate government."

But Calhoun failed to generate enough of his own spirit among others, and he and his supporters backed down when President Andrew Jackson threatened force. Calhoun's proposed Nullification Act was tabled for good, but the resentments on which it was based grew like an anxious Topsy for nearly three decades. In October 1860 Alexander Stephens, a Georgian, voiced a sentiment which could hardly have been more to the point. The South, he declared, could "make better terms out of the Union than in it." It was an openly known fact in Charleston that if Abraham Lincoln, an enemy of slavery, were elected to the Presidency, South Carolina would secede—a dramatically simple solution to a most complex problem.

The economic, moral and emotional forces that were to culminate in war were abetted by personalities of a curiously unfortunate flavor. There, in 1860, in Washington, was President James Buchanan, elected

by a substantial majority in 1856 with the support of
fourteen of the fifteen slave states. He was wavering,
indecisive and naïve. And in his Cabinet, in the sensitive post of Secretary of War, sat John B. Floyd,
former Governor of South Carolina, who exercised an
almost hypnotic influence over his chief and intrigued,
behind his back, for Southern independence. Floyd was
not a decent man of conviction who happened to dis-
agree with his President; he was a sophisticated self-
seeker, a manipulator, and he had several close associates and supporters with him in the Government:
Secretary of the Treasury Howell Cobb of Georgia,
Secretary of the Navy Isaac Toucey, Secretary of the
Interior Jacob Thompson, and William H. Trescot,
acting Secretary of State. These men, with Floyd,
were prepared to aid the Southern cause, at the risk of
disloyalty to their posts, their President, the Federal
Government. Buchanan, either too ignorant or too
anxious, seemed unaware that in his Cabinet were five
men dead-set against the North. As his term drew to a
close the President, sensing that he would not be up to
the demands of a mounting crisis, attempted to avoid
an immediate showdown; what happened after he left
office would not be his responsibility.

Then there was the senator from Texas, Louis T.
Wigfall, an idealist so carried away by his own fervor
that he boasted "Give us till November to drill our
men, and we shall be irresistible"—blithely overlook-
ing the fact that the South had no factories, mills or
armories.

And there was William Lloyd Garrison of Boston,
whose anti-slavery feelings so overwhelmed him that
on one occasion in 1854 he set fire to a copy of the
Constitution, branding it a "covenant with death and

an agreement with Hell," making even his abolitionist audience squirm.

All over the country emotions reached an uncontrol-
lable pitch; the valid economic grievances of the South
and the equally valid moral stand of the North were
aggravated by a dangerous excess of feelings and men
who exploited them. Lincoln's election would mean
that the territories of Kansas and Nebraska would be
admitted to the Union not as slave but as free states—
the single biggest issue of the campaign between Lincoln and Stephen A. Douglas.

At this crucial moment the Governor of South Carolina, William H. Gist, initiated a concerted movement for secession. On October 5, 1860, a special
messenger left the executive office in the State Capitol
at Columbia with a circular letter from Gist, destined
for the governors of the eight Cotton States. Its contents seem remarkably clearheaded and coolly decisive.
Gist asked the governors for an "interchange of opinions" on the question of secession, should Lincoln be
elected. "If a single state secedes," he wrote, South
Carolina "will follow her. If no other states take
the lead, South Carolina will secede alone, if she has
the assurance that she will soon be followed by another or other states." He admitted that this proposal
was his own and did not yet have legislative sanction.
The replies started arriving on October 18. North
Carolina was first, stating that she did not deem Lincoln's election sufficient cause for secession. The next
two answers were more positive but still cautious.
Governor Moore of Alabama promised that although
his state would not go it alone, she would secede if
one or two states joined her. "If any state moves,"
wrote Governor Pettus, "I think Mississippi will go

with her." The Governor of Louisiana wrote Gist that "I would not advise the secession of my state and I will add that I do not think that the people of Louisiana will, ultimately, decide in favor of that course."

On October 31, Georgia's Governor Brown answered, "The people of Georgia will wait for some overt act. There are many friends of the Union in the state, and others who, from interest, look with suspicion upon the threatened movement." A month later, Florida came back with wholehearted support for secession: "Florida is ready to wheel in line with the gallant Palmetto State," her Governor, Perry, boasted to Gist. Governor Hicks of Maryland stood pat for the Union. Virginia was still doubtful. The score was three for, three against, and two on the fence—and, of course, Gist for.

While Gist actively worked for secession in Columbia, Floyd was busy sending arms and ammunition in excess of requirements to the Southern states, anticipating approaching war and, privately, adding to a list of those whom he was sure he could count on, in government and army service, to fall in with the secession "army." Working overtime, he deliberately withheld from Buchanan any information about the operation of the War Department, and he attempted to bypass the Army's Chief of Staff, seventy-four-year-old Lieutenant General Winfield Scott.

Scott was fiercely loyal to the Union and alert to the dangers of Southern insurrection. "We are now in such a state that a dogfight might cause the gutters of the Capital to run with blood," he told one of his aides. He was six feet five inches tall and weighed three hundred pounds; when he appeared on the street

in his plumed hat and blue uniform with gold braid
and brass buttons he seemed like a one-man parade.
Yet this great hulk of a man was now full of years
as well as honors; he suffered from dropsy and ver-
tigo and could no longer ride a horse or work for
more than a short spell at a desk. He was compelled
to spend long hours resting on the sofa in his Washington office. A faraway look would sometimes come
into his eyes and he would recall, "I was three years
old when the Constitution was adopted."

He was the head of the Army; he had spent his
entire life in the service of his country; he was a hero
to the people, who nicknamed him "Old Fuss and
Feathers." Yet Buchanan was too timid to listen to
him, and Floyd refused to. On October 31 Scott suggested that Floyd send a circular to all Federal forts
warning the commanders to be on guard against sudden surprise assault. The Secretary of War ignored the
advice. And Buchanan hastily backed away from
Scott's warning that unless the Federal government
acted, the South Carolinians "would have the game
in their hands."

James Buchanan, worn down by a sense of his own
inadequacy, resorted to tears when he begged strangers
to help him save the country from "bloody, fratri-
cidal war." In his last months as President, Buchanan
ceased action utterly; he rejected Scott's further plea
to send men and arms to protect the Federal forts in
Southern territory against possible seizure. Floyd and
his colleagues in the Cabinet naturally took advantage
of their chief's weakness.

On November 7, the news of Lincoln's election
broke over Charleston like an exploding shell. Her citizens went wild. Minutemen sprang into ready-for-

action companies. Vigilance committees formed. Men rushed to buy rifles and ammunition. Street-corner orators openly called for secession while Palmetto flags waved defiantly over their heads. Restaurants and stores called "National" changed their names to "Southern" or "Palmetto." Secession fanaticism took hold. At the Charleston Theater on Meeting Street, Charleston Volunteers performed drills and flourishes on stage for audiences, who preferred their maneuvers to the songs of the great visiting opera star, Adelina Patti. Bonfires roared and crackled in parks and squares; Charleston declared a holiday.

And in the State Capitol at Columbia, a member of the United States Congress, W. W. Boyce, arose in the legislative chamber and shouted with inciting illogic, "The way to create a revolution is to start it. To submit to Lincoln's election is to consent to death!"

"No such
orders have
been given"

As Charleston whipped itself into a frenzy of resentment and military preparations, the ring of Federal forts in the harbor took on a double significance: as symbols of the Union and as instruments of power which might be turned against the city and close the port, should secession become a reality.

Squatting threateningly in the center of the harbor at its narrowest part was Fort Sumter, a pentagonal structure resting on a man-made island of sea shells and granite refuse chips from Northern quarries. Walls fifty feet high and from eight to twelve feet thick rose from its base. It was named after Thomas Sumter, the Gamecock of the Revolution, who had harassed and baffled the British during the Carolina campaign. The first plans for the fort were drawn up in 1827 after a survey of the Eastern coastline had emphasized both the vulnerability and the strategic and commercial importance of Charleston. In conjunction with two other forts in the harbor, Sumter's purpose was to provide complete protection for the city from any hostile ship that might attempt an approach. Charleston lies on a tongue of land between the Ashley and the Cooper rivers, and from their meeting place to the open sea are four miles of harbor made treacherous by small islands, reefs and shallows. Fort Sumter and her companion defenses, Castle Pinckney and Fort Moultrie on Sullivan's Island, were designed to make those waters more treacherous and more forbidding for any potential invader.

From the time work was begun in 1829, the construction of Sumter was a series of encounters with natural and human obstacles. The tides in the harbor prevented continuous work on the foundation, and epidemics of yellow fever plagued the crews intermittently. While the foundations were still being laid, trouble of another kind put a temporary stop to the work. This was a question of land ownership, raised by a citizen of Charleston who claimed to have a state grant to the land in the harbor. When the issue was finally resolved, it established the fact that the United States Government could and did own 125 acres of harbor "land." The work went ahead.

By November 1860, despite over thirty years' work and the expenditure of nearly a million dollars, Fort Sumter was still unfinished and unfit for service. Of a possible complement of 140 guns of heavy caliber, only fifteen were ready for use. The barracks were unfinished, in no condition to receive a garrison. On the open parade ground stood flimsy wooden shacks erected by the workmen for toolsheds and storehouses. The parade ground was also littered with an inde-

scribable confusion of sand and rough masonry, un-
mounted guns with their wooden carriages, shot and
shell, piles of flagstones, coils of rope, blocks and
tackle, loose timbers, kegs and boxes and all the debris
of a fortification still building.

The other harbor fortifications—Castle Pinckney
and Fort Moultrie—were equally unready for emergency. Pinckney was an impressive fort with mount-
ings for many heavy guns and with walls six feet
thick. As conceived, it was an ideal fort except for
one curious structural anomaly: because there were no
windows in the lower tier, the overwhelming reverberation of the cannon could quickly force the gunners
from their stations. When garrisoned and in condition,
Pinckney still could have been a pistol pointed right
at Charleston's head, but in 1860 it was more like
some picturesquely dilapidated relic from another time.
Casemates were cracked; grass grew between the flagstones. It was only because of the peculiar devotion of
an old ordnance sergeant, who lived at the fort with
his wife and daughter, that the guns had not rusted
away into scrap; he had spent countless hours polish-
ing the barrels and round shot, and he had tried to
save the fort from being entirely reclaimed by nature.

Fort Moultrie, on Sullivan's Island, had seen duty
during the Revolution when its guns had guarded
Charleston against the British fleet. Now rebuilt, it
was in effect a huge sea battery which lacked cover
for its guns. Fort Moultrie Military Reservation
swept across Sullivan's Island like a waist belt of
moderate width; the fort itself was the buckle. If a
hostile vessel started up the main channel entrance of
the harbor she would be caught between the crossfire
of Sumter and Moultrie—if the forts happened to be

prepared. Moultrie was not equipped with necessary armaments; in addition, she was easily accessible, for there were large piles of sand against her walls, swept there by winds and tides, and any child could have entered her. Moultrie's peaceful neglect came to an end when Congress, advised of her inadequacies and fearful of war, appropriated money for repairs, including removal of the sand. Captain James G. Foster of the Corps of Engineers was ordered to Charleston to take over the work at Moultrie and at Sumter as well.

If a soldier had to be on duty at all during the summer of 1860, Moultrie, though militarily unprepared, was still a choice post. Sullivan's Island was the summer residence of many of Charleston's best families, who entertained the Federal troops and mingled with them, promenaded the parapets almost daily, attended Fort Moultrie's band concerts, and in general behaved with hospitality and charm. As the season extended into October, however, this fashionable set began to realize that there was a widening gulf between them and the Federal soldiers who had drawn this pleasant duty. The Charlestonians became especially kind and solicitous to the enlisted men, who, it was hoped, might be wooed from their original allegiance in case war should break out between North and South.

One afternoon some of Moultrie's enlisted men on pass were present at a barbecue for a local political candidate and shared the liquor and the mounds of food set out on tables in the fine fall air. After supper, when the chairman of the affair had risen to his feet and begun his speech, a soldier, whose judgment had been blunted by drink, spotted what seemed to be the

only slice of uneaten ham left at the supper; it was
on the chairman's plate. The soldier climbed onto the
table and, picking his way among the dishes, walked
its entire length, reached the chairman's place, bent
over, picked up the piece of meat, popped it into his
mouth and retreated down the length of the table,
chewing. A gasp of anger rose from the crowd. In
a flash the chairman drew his revolver and shouted,
"I'll shoot the first man who interferes with that
soldier!" No one moved except the soldier, who
walked off, unperturbed and apparently satisfied. An
enlisted man was only a mercenary, the Charlestonians reasoned, and, with forbearance and generosity,
carried even to the point of self-abasement, they might
win him over.

The Commandant of Fort Moultrie Military Reservation was Colonel James Gardiner, an aging veteran of the Mexican War who was anything but an
alarmist. While the city of Charleston was roiling
with imminent rebellion, Gardiner went about his routine duties at the fort with no more vigilance or
anxiety than he would show on any peaceful day. It
was not until October that any steps at all were
taken to prepare for a possible emergency, and then it
was not Gardiner but his engineer officer, Foster, who
took them: Foster sent an urgent message, with Gardiner's approval, to the Chief of Ordnance in Washington requesting that the civilian workmen at Fort
Sumter be issued small arms in order to protect Government property. Foster was promised forty muskets
for the laborers. Gardiner himself finally woke up to
the repeated pleas of his officers and recommended to
Washington that trained recruits be sent to Fort
Moultrie and Castle Pinckney.

But by November 7 nothing had actually been accomplished; even the promised muskets had not been delivered from the U.S. arsenal in Charleston. The apathetic Colonel Gardiner, slow-moving and half functioning, became sufficiently aroused by intimations of trouble to authorize another attempt to secure supplies, both ammunition and food, for Fort Moultrie. He ordered Captain Truman Seymour to set out for the arsenal with a group of soldiers in the precautionary disguise of civilians. The disguises failed, as a spy from the jittery population of Sullivan's Island sent warning of the men's approach ahead to the city. When Seymour and his men tied up at the Charleston wharf, a suspicious crowd, murmuring with animosity, stood waiting for them. Hampered by difficulty in obtaining carts, Seymour was able to get only one cart loaded before the tide slipped out to sea, grounding the schooner. The soldiers had to spend the night in the city.

Governor Gist took advantage of this convenient delay and wired to acting Secretary of State Trescot to inquire if Seymour's little expedition had been authorized in Washington. Trescot went straight to Secretary of War Floyd, who told him: "Telegraph back at once. Say that you have seen me, that no such orders have been given, and none shall be given under any circumstances." Seymour was completely blocked. The next morning he and his men set sail for Moultrie with a safe cargo of food and other supplies— but with neither ammunition nor guns.

This near incident made Floyd realize that things were happening in Charleston over which he ought to have more control. He also wanted an eyewitness account of the true state of Federal fortifications and morale. Wasting little time, on the night of November 9 he summoned Major Fitz-John Porter of the Adjutant General's office. Porter was to go to Charleston, inspect the forts and submit his report. A loyal Union man with a mediocre military mind, Porter spent two days on a thorough tour of the fortifications. Moultrie, he reported, was in such a poor state of preparedness that any real emergency could wipe it out; Gardiner had allowed a deplorable lack of discipline and guns to weaken the fort to the point of uselessness. Fort Sumter, Porter advised, should probably not be occupied at the present time. He gave as his reasons the unfinished state of the fort, its occupation by local workmen whose loyalty was suspect, and his personal opinion that it was only a moderately strategic installation—something of an understatement in view of developing circumstances. Castle Pinckney, Porter concluded, was too run down to be of much use and it too should not be occupied.

Porter was unwittingly telling Floyd exactly what he wanted to hear, and the Secretary must have been pleased. But there was still the problem of Gardiner, who was enfeebled by age but unquestionably loyal to the Union. The choice was Floyd's: Would he rather see a loyal incompetent commanding Moultrie or a good soldier who seemed to be "safe" for Floyd and the Southern cause? Floyd chose the second, or thought he had, in the person of Major Robert Anderson, a Kentuckian by birth and a Virginian by ancestry, a man in whom he had "great confidence." Accordingly, Floyd issued an order to General Winfield Scott to replace Gardiner with Anderson and, for good measure, to put Colonel Ben Huger, a Carolinian, another man whom Floyd felt he could trust (and with reason, for Huger subsequently joined the Confederate Army), in charge of the Charleston arsenal.

Floyd's sphere of influence now extended into the heart of Charleston, and his tactics were no longer merely defensive or delaying: he was creating the situation. He was the dominant member of a busy cabal whose machinations had, by this time, such a driving force behind them that a showdown was inevitable.

"Keep a sharp lookout upon them"

The fifty-six-year-old veteran read the words again: "By command of General Scott, Major Robert Anderson, First Artillery, will proceed to Fort Moultrie and immediately relieve Brevet Colonel John J. Gardiner, Lieutenant Colonel, First Artillery, in command thereof." The major was unhappily aware of the urgency and implications of these orders.

Anderson was on temporary leave with his family at Soldier's Retreat, the Kentucky plantation named by his father, Richard Clough Anderson, a lieutenant colonel in the Continental Army. The major's wife was Elizabeth Clinch, daughter of a general, the mother of five children, a Georgia-born beauty. It was her background and Anderson's planter and slave-owning status that probably led Floyd to select him for the post at Moultrie. But Floyd was dead wrong about Anderson. Despite his private interests and private opinions, loyalty to his officer's oath dominated his life and career. "The selection of the place in which we were born was not an act of our own volition," Anderson once declared to a fellow officer, a Southerner, "but when we took the oath of allegiance to our Government it was an act of our manhood, and that oath we cannot break." That statement placed a stamp of integrity on all his actions and delineated the problem and the choices soon to confront him.

He was deeply troubled by the tensions which threatened to divide the country, and although he felt that war was inevitable, he hoped the wayward states could, at some future time, be won back by conciliation and justice. Should his native state of Kentucky secede from the Union, Anderson hoped to be a spectator rather than a combatant; he would take his family to Europe for the duration of the contest. He could well afford the luxury of this solution, for in his own right and also through his wife he was, by the standards of the time, a rich man. His private income and holdings made an ironic contrast with the $64 a month plus subsistence a major's rank entitled him to.

He was a religious man and looked like an itinerant family preacher. But he had been a soldier too long not to have adopted the fatalism of his profession. "We will do our duty"—these were his parting words to Elizabeth as he began his journey to Charleston.

It took him five days to get there by slow train. On November 20 he caught the 3:30 boat to Sullivan's Island, assumed command of Moultrie with a minimum of ceremony, and began an inspection of the military installations in the harbor. Captain Foster, the senior engineer officer, accompanied him on his rounds.

By November 23 Anderson was sufficiently familiar with the military situation of the area to make his first official report to Washington. He had seen at once that Fort Sumter was "the key to the entrance of the harbor; its guns command this work, Moultrie, and could drive out its occupants." He recommended that Sumter be garrisoned immediately. Castle Pinckney, too, should be occupied by two officers and thirty men to insure the safety of itself and of Moultrie. "The Charlestonians," he reasoned, "will not venture to attack this place, when they see that their city is at the mercy of the commander of Castle Pinckney." Anderson requested that twenty-six civilian workmen be put to work repairing Pinckney's cracked and crumbling walls and casemates.

Anderson's communiqués from Moultrie reached Floyd through Adjutant General Samuel Cooper, whose sympathies were much the same as the Secretary's; Cooper later stepped into the post of Chief-of-Staff of the Confederate States' Provisional Army. Together, Cooper and Floyd sent a blanket refusal to every one of Anderson's requests and asked instead for information about "the present state of command," exactly what Anderson had just sent them. Floyd indicated that he was concerned with Moultrie's potential in case of attack and suggested that "in view of maintaining troops ready for efficient action and defense, it might be advisable to employ reliable persons not connected with the military service for purposes of fatigue and police." Anderson, with dexterity and clear logic, avoided complying: excitement in Charleston was at too high a pitch to risk hiring Southerners for such a job. Moreover, the garrison had recently been "openly and publicly threatened." Anderson's reasoned refusal to carry out Floyd's suggestion signaled the beginning of an implicit struggle between the two men.

Granted that Anderson was not the man Floyd hoped he was (and happily for the Union cause), he was a good and experienced soldier who had seen action and who had qualities of leadership. His military career began when President James Monroe in 1821 appointed him to West Point, where he received his second lieutenant's commission. After a short nonmilitary stint as private secretary to his half brother, Richard C. Anderson, Jr., first United States Minister to Colombia, Anderson got back in uniform and in 1826 served as an artillery instructor at Fortress Monroe in Virginia. Six years later he saw his first action in the Black Hawk War. As Assistant Inspector General on the staff of General Henry Atkinson, Anderson mustered in a young volunteer named Abraham Lincoln who commanded a brigade called the Clary Grove Boys; these ruffians did their fighting in barrooms and did not experience a single day of action. Anderson mustered out an unseasoned Lincoln at the end of the war.

In 1833 Anderson received his first lieutenant's commission, and after two years at Fort Constitution in New Hampshire he returned to West Point as Assistant Instructor of Artillery. Among his students were William Tecumseh Sherman and P. G. T. Beauregard, who years later was to oppose Anderson across the waters of Charleston Harbor. But in the peaceful thirties, Beauregard and Anderson were anything but adversaries; Beauregard considered Anderson his favorite instructor.

Again, Anderson was called on to take part in a minor conflict: the Florida War of 1837. This time he served as aide-de-camp to General Winfield Scott, fighting against the Seminoles. Promoted to Assistant Adjutant General and brevetted captain on Scott's staff, he spent the subsequent three years in skirmishes with the Indians.

Anderson knew Fort Moultrie; he had spent a year there in garrison just before the Mexican War, in which, as a captain, he took part in the battles of Vera Cruz and Molino del Ray. At Chapultepec he caught a Mexican bullet in his shoulder after a brilliant show of heroism. He received a citation for "meritorious and gallant conduct" and was brevetted major.

Anderson was familiar with the techniques of warfare from direct experience. He was regarded as a hero of the Mexican War; he was well and justifiably liked as a man of serene spirit and sympathy. A tall man with instinctive military carriage and a handsome face, Anderson was, at fifty-six, looking forward to his earned retirement with quiet pleasure when the biggest war of all caught up with him and changed his plans.

Five days after his first urgent request to Floyd, Anderson again sent the Secretary a message emphasizing that Moultrie could be protected only if Pinckney were garrisoned and adding that in his opinion Sumter should have been occupied first. Anderson's message crossed one from Cooper to him advising him that workmen would be sent to start repairs on Castle Pinckney. Apparently Floyd had decided that the old fort had better be in fighting condition when the Charlestonians came to take it over. Anderson was ordered, in the same communiqué, to direct anything he had to say to the War Department or to Floyd directly, thus fulfilling Floyd's plan to by-pass General Scott.

Meanwhile, workmen were busy trying to bring Forts Moultrie and Sumter out of rusting chaos, and late in November Anderson was able to report to Washington that Moultrie would soon be in working order.

At first, Charlestonians vacationing on Sullivan's Island paid the activity little heed, but as the threat of war increased they began to regard repairs as "aggression" and told Anderson so, warning him that as soon as South Carolina seceded, the state would demand that the forts be evacuated of Federal troops. They threatened also that no men or stores would be allowed to reach him from Charleston. This aggressive talk reflected the warlike activities going on now in the city. All able-bodied men were enrolling in military companies and drilling for attack—on Fort Moultrie. Northern manufacturers were deluged by orders for firearms, epaulets, gold braid, swords, military decorations and fancy fittings generally. An article greatly in demand was the South Carolina flag, which, on a white ground, showed a palmetto tree in the center and a red star in the upper right-hand corner. Toward the end of November a false rumor that six hundred Federal troops were coming to man the forts in the harbor whipped the temper of the city into near hysteria.

On December 6, a desperate Anderson suggested to Floyd that in view of the fact that Sumter, "a tempting prize," was not yet garrisoned, all work should be stopped there: "the guns certainly ought not to be mounted, as they might be turned upon me at

Moultrie." If stores and reinforcements did not reach him soon Anderson admitted that his men could not distinguish themselves by holding out for long.

Robert Anderson deluged the War Department by day; at night he wrote troubled and revealing letters to his friends. To Robert N. Gourdin of Charleston he expressed his anxieties in this way:

> You need no assurance from me that, although I am exerting myself to make this little work as strong as possible and to put my handful of men in the highest state of discipline, no one will do more than *I am willing to do to keep the South in the right and to avoid the shedding of blood*. You may be somewhat surprised at the sentiment I express, being a soldier, but I think an appeal to arms and brute force is unbecoming the age in which we live. Would to God that the time had come when there should be no war, and that religion and peace should reign throughout the world.

To a Trenton, New Jersey, rector, Anderson described the military dilemma he feared he might have to face:

> A word or two about my position, and so on. As soon as I had time to inspect my position and ascertain the feeling and temper of the people here, I found that to enable me to comply with my orders to defend this fort, it was absolutely necessary that more troops and ordnance stores must be sent. And I recommended that they should be sent at once. The Government has declined for prudential reasons to send them, and I must now do the best I can. This fort is a very weak one in its capacity of being defended; it is surrounded by

houses that I cannot burn or destroy until I am
certain that I am to be attacked, and I shall not be
certain of it until the South Carolinians are in possession; but I have so little ammunition that I cannot waste it in destroying houses. And again,
within one hundred and sixty yards of the walls
are piles of sand-hills, some of them higher than
our fort, which will give the best and safest shelter
for sharp-shooters, who may pick off in a short
time our band of sixty men—all we have.

It would not have taken a particularly sensitive
man to see that the situation in this important area
was becoming alarming. Anderson renewed his request
for additional troops and vessels of war. His request
went unanswered. Anderson, frustrated, put it bluntly
to Floyd: would the Federal Government surrender
the forts in the harbor in the event South Carolina
seceded?

Floyd and Cooper could no longer safely ignore
Anderson's persistent requests for troops and instructions; if Floyd failed to act it would surely get
around that he was ignoring his own man in Charleston. Floyd felt his hand being forced and decided to
act.

Bringing the question of Charleston's defense into
the open, Floyd arranged to have it discussed at
lengthy Cabinet meetings and to get the Secretaries to
agree to have him handle the situation in whatever
way he deemed best. His tactics had been successful.
The only answers the hamstrung Anderson got were
soothing communications from Cooper: "It is believed
from information thought to be reliable, that an attack will *not* be made on your command, and the
Secretary has only to refer to his correspondence with

you to caution you that, should his convictions unhappily prove untrue, your actions must be such as to be free from the charge of initiating a collision."

Floyd now resolved to rely on the services of another messenger, in this instance Major Don Carlos Buell of the Adjutant General's Department. Buell was called in by Floyd on December 7 and instructed to proceed to Charleston and, like Porter, report to Floyd on the military situation there. During the interview, it became clear to Buell that Floyd wanted Anderson committed to a policy of defense only. Hardly any mention was made of reinforcements. Floyd wanted nothing committed to writing, neither his instructions to Buell nor Buell's findings. Buell left the Secretary's office slightly puzzled as to the ultimate implications of his mission.

On December 10, while Buell was on his way to Charleston, President Buchanan received five delegates from South Carolina in his office. These men—Generals M. L. Bonham and John McQueen and Messrs. William Porcher Miles, William W. Boyce, and Lawrence M. Keitt—had come with the express mission of obtaining a pledge from Buchanan that the *status quo* in Charleston Harbor would be maintained. To this end they presented him with a paper they had jointly written and signed:

> We now express to you our strong convictions that neither the constituted authority nor any body of the people of the state of South Carolina will either attack or molest the United States forts in the harbor of Charleston, provided that no reinforcements shall be sent into those forts and their relative military status shall remain as at present.

Buchanan agreed to give them his oral pledge, but he would not sign any paper to that effect. "After all, this is a matter of honor among gentlemen," he said. "I do not know that any paper or writing is necessary. We understand each other."

The delegates left with the impression that the President, despite his insistence on a gentlemen's agreement only, intended to stand by his pledge not to alter the balance of power in Charleston Harbor. It was not until the end of December that Buchanan was forced to realize that he had no right to make any pledge, whether orally or in writing, that would be binding on the Government and that he should not have recognized the delegates as having any official status. In imposing conditions on the way the Government managed its own properties and installations, South Carolina was pushing an advantage with a weak President, whose only policy was the negative one of averting conflict until his term was over, and with a Federal Government made pliable and impotent by the absurd lack of any united policy.

On December 11, Buell was being welcomed at Moultrie by Anderson. They spent that day together, touring the forts. Although he had planned to return to Washington when his inspection was complete, Buell was persuaded by Anderson to spend the night at Moultrie in Anderson's quarters. If Buell had left when he originally intended, he never would have set down in writing his interpretations of Floyd's instruction. Disregarding Floyd's injunction, he told Anderson, "You ought to have written evidence of these instructions."

Buell's interpretation of Floyd's intent was put in this form:

MEMORANDUM OF VERBAL INSTRUCTIONS TO MAJOR ANDERSON, FIRST ARTILLERY, COMMANDING FORT MOULTRIE, SOUTH CAROLINA:

You are aware of the great anxiety of the Secretary of War, that a collision of the troops with the people of this State shall be avoided, and of his studied determination to pursue a course with reference to the military force and forts in this harbor which shall guard against such collision. He has, therefore, carefully abstained from increasing the force at this point, or taking any measures which might add to the present excited state of the public mind, or which would throw any doubts on the confidence he feels that South Carolina will not attempt by violence to obtain possession of the public works or interfere with their occupancy. But as the counsel and acts of rash and impulsive persons may possibly disappoint these expectations of the Government, he deems it proper that you should be prepared with instructions to meet so unhappy a contingency. He has, therefore, directed me verbally to give you such instructions.

You are carefully to avoid every act which would needlessly tend to provoke aggression; and for that reason you are not, without evidence and imminent necessity, to take up any position which could be construed into the assumption of a hostile attitude. But you are to hold possession of the forts in this harbor, and if attacked, you are to defend yourself to the last extremity. The smallness of your force will not permit you to occupy more than one of the three forts, but an attack on or an attempt to take possession of any one of them will be regarded as an act of hostility, and you may then put your command into either of them

which you deem most proper, to increase its power
of resistance. You are also authorized to take
similar steps whenever you have tangible evidence
of a design to proceed to a hostile act.

Buell handed the memorandum to Anderson, keeping a copy for himself. "This is all I am authorized
to do," he said, "but my personal advice is that you
do not let the opportunity to occupy Sumter escape
you." Buell unwittingly made himself a pivotal character in the complex drama: his written instructions,
running contrary to Buchanan's pledge, were to em-
barrass the President, confound Floyd, and give Anderson the go-ahead signal to act as he thought best.

Buell stayed over yet another night. The next day
was Sunday and he spent it in Charleston, seeing in
the demonstrations and in the temper of the people
evidence of a settled purpose to secede and to have the
forts for the South. Buell and Anderson were in
accord on every point: Moultrie was untenable, and
unless Sumter were occuped by Federal troops it would
be seized by the people, with or without sanction from
the authorities.

In Washington, Buell reported his findings to Floyd
orally, but on his way out of the Secretary's office
he left a copy of his memorandum with Drinkard, the
chief clerk at the War Department. Whether Floyd
was shown the document when it was filed or some
days later is in doubt.

After Buell had left, the following item appeared
in the Charleston *Mercury:* "Major Buell and several
other officers of the Army have been sent to look
after the forts. Keep a sharp lookout for them. They
were sent for no good to us. See that they make no

changes in the distribution of soldiers, so as to put them all in Fort Sumter. That would be dangerous to us."

On December 14 the New York *Herald* reported that the garrison at Moultrie "is evidently in dread of an attack and is preparing night and day for a desperate resistance in such event."

CHAPTER
FOUR
| "The Union
is dissolved"

In the person of Francis Pickens, the newly elected
Governor of South Carolina, Robert Anderson now
had another antagonist who would use every pressure
and device to destroy him. Planter, local politician,
United States congressman, diplomat, lawyer, Pickens
was a man of talent and ambition. He had been con-
tent with his post as Minister to Russia until news
reached him of the mounting tension between his state
and the Federal Government. Determined to become
a leader of the pro-slavery forces, he asked for his
recall and returned home.

A portly man of medium height, Pickens managed to make an imposing appearance despite watery
eyes and broad, flabby features. He had a pompous
manner and an annoying tendency to regale his visi-
tors with a lecture on the vicious differences between
capital and labor in the North, a lecture he had

practiced on the Czar of Russia. Yet even those who laughed at his pretensions and eccentricities could not deny that he was a determined man and a master of intrigue. To the architects of secession—Rhett, Yancey, and Barnwell—Pickens appeared to have the ideal qualifications for governor: he was experienced, he was forceful in his support of the Calhoun doctrines, he was crafty. On December 14, 1860, having openly committed himself to the stand that "South Carolina has no alternative but to secede," he was elected to fill the chair vacated by Gist.

The ensuing months were to dramatize the antithetic qualities of Pickens and Anderson. Where Anderson was cautious and deliberating, Pickens was rash and impulsive, his zeal often stronger than his discretion. Pickens was an experienced and professional diplomat, skilled in legal subtleties and expediency; Anderson put his faith in open statements and common-sense rules of thumb. But while Anderson was a professional soldier, trained by both battlefield and textbook, Pickens wanted to add the title of general to his honors and he did not have the talent for it. Pickens was kind and hospitable by nature, but he was driven by a hunger for personal glory; Anderson was calm and self-effacing. Both men believed in slavery and in the Southern "cause." But Pickens would use any means to gain the end of Southern sovereignty, while Anderson subordinated his personal feelings and political beliefs to the duty that he owed his country.

Early in the afternoon of December 17, Pickens returned to his office at the State Capitol in Columbia, 113 miles northwest of Charleston. That morning he had attended the first meeting of the South Carolina Convention, and, like the other delegates, he had expected that by the end of the day an ordinance of secession would have been drafted and unanimously approved, an expectation frustrated by the announcement that a smallpox epidemic was raging through the city. The convention soberly agreed on the wisdom of adjourning to Charleston. Now, in the discontented time before the convention would take up its work again, Pickens wrote a letter to President Buchanan in Washington and entrusted it to Major D. H. Hamilton of the South Carolina Volunteers. Hamilton was ordered to deliver it to the President personally:

(STRICTLY CONFIDENTIAL)
Columbia, December 17th, 1860

MY DEAR SIR:

With a sincere desire to prevent a collision of force, I have thought proper to address you directly and truthfully on points of deep and immediate interest.

I am authentically informed that the forts in Charleston Harbor are now being thoroughly prepared to turn, with effect, their guns upon the interior of the city.

Jurisdiction was ceded by this State expressly for the purpose of external defense from foreign invasion, and not with any view that they should be turned upon the State. In an ordinary case of mob rebellion, perhaps it might be proper to prepare them for sudden outbreak. But when the people of the State, in sovereign convention assembled, determine to resume their original power of separate and independent sovereignty, the whole question is changed, and it is no longer an act of rebellion.

I, therefore, most respectfully urge that all

work on the forts be put to a stop for the present, and that no more force may be ordered there. The regular Convention of the people of the State of South Carolina, legally and properly called, under our constitution, is now in session, deliberating upon the gravest and most momentous questions, and the excitement of the great masses of people is great, under a sense of deep wrongs and a profound necessity of doing something to preserve the peace and safety of the State.

To spare the effusion of blood, which no human power may be able to prevent, I earnestly beg your immediate consideration of all points I call to your attention. It is not improbable that under orders from the Commandant, or, perhaps from the Commander in Chief of the Army, the alterations and defenses of those posts are progressing without the knowledge of yourself or the Secretary of War.

I would most respectfully, and from a sincere devotion to public peace, request that you would allow me to send a small force, not exceeding twenty-five men and an officer, to take possession of Fort Sumter immediately in order to give a feeling of safety to the community. There are no United States troops in that fort whatever, or perhaps only four or five at present, besides some additional workmen or laborers, lately employed to put the guns in order.

I need not go into particulars, for urgent reasons will force themselves readily upon your consideration. If something of the kind not be done I cannot answer for the consequences.

That afternoon, while Pickens' messenger began his journey to Washington, Captain Foster left Fort

Moultrie and went into Charleston. His purpose was to procure from the arsenal two hoists for mounting heavy guns. But when he discovered that Colonel Huger was absent, Foster saw the opportunity for a desperate stratagem. Reminding the military store-keeper of the War Department's unfilled order for forty muskets, Foster was able to convince him to comply with the order and send the muskets along with the hoists. Foster stayed long enough to oversee the loading of both hoists and muskets and he returned to Moultrie.

The complete lack of security measures again had immediate effect. News of the removal of the muskets sped through Charleston, already overexcited by the hope of momentary secession; and the hapless store-keeper was compelled to send an urgent note to Foster demanding the return of the muskets and prophesying direst results if they were not returned. Foster could only answer that he was willing to refer the matter to Washington. But here he was anticipated by a tel-egram sent to Trescot by Pickens' aide, J. J. Petti-grew: "Great excitement prevails. Telegraph to have the arms instantly returned, or a collision may occur at any moment. Three days will determine in con-vention war or peace, and this act not instantly coun-termanded by telegraph will be decisive. Not a mo-ment's time should be lost."

Trescot received this telegram late at night; it was clearly important enough for him to awaken Floyd, who lost no time in authorizing his chief clerk to send a wire in his name to Captain Foster ordering him to return the arms instantly, an order which Ander-son, after conferring with Foster, had already given. The next day the guns were back in the arsenal; an-

other attempt to build up the Federal forces to minimum defensive strength had been thwarted.

"The Governor says he is glad of your dispatch,
for otherwise there would have been imminent danger," Pettigrew wired back to Trescot on December
18. Pickens had arrived in Charleston at his temporary
Executive Office in the white colonnaded Charleston
Hotel on Meeting Street. Uncertainty and haste per-
vaded the place. On the doors of the various offices
were pasted crudely scribbled signs—"Attorney
General of the State," "Adjutant General's Department," "Quartermaster General's Department."
Through open doors Pickens could see men in uniform busily writing orders and dispatches, every now
and then turning toward the brass spittoons within
easy reach.

Pickens immediately acted to prevent any further
attempt to strengthen Anderson's position. He ordered
the steamer *Nina,* carrying a detachment of the Washington Light Infantry, to shuttle back and forth between Moultrie and Sumter and stop any vessel suspected of carrying Federal troops. Pickens consoli-
dated his strategy by sending Colonel John Green to
Fortress Monroe at Norfolk, the main base of
United States Army operations, to find out what he
could about any contemplated troop movements for
Charleston. He also engaged a Mr. Charles Norris,
reputed head of the Secessionist Minutemen of Norfolk, to set up a spy system at the Navy Yard there.
Acting with speed and decision, Pickens seemed to
have got off to a good start in his battle of wits
with Anderson.

On December 20 Major Hamilton arrived in
Washington and with the help of Trescot was given

an appointment with Buchanan to deliver Pickens' demand for Sumter. The President received Hamilton and Trescot in the library of the White House. After reading Pickens' letter, Buchanan asked Hamilton when an answer was expected. "As soon as possible, Mr. President," Hamilton said. "I am returning to Charleston tomorrow morning." It would be impossible to give an answer in so short a time, Buchanan declared: Could he have more time? "Yes, until tomorrow evening," Hamilton answered.

"Mr. President," Hamilton went on, "I am aware of the contents of that letter, and think that if you would accept them, it would greatly facilitate negotiations between my Government and the United States." Buchanan replied that he would keep this in mind while considering his answer. As Hamilton and Trescot began to leave the room, their interview at an end, Buchanan handed the letter to Trescot and asked him to read it and return it later.

Trescot was quick to take action. He conferred with Senators Jefferson Davis and John Slidell and with two members of the South Carolina delegation, Bonham and McQueen. All agreed that Pickens' demand for Sumter could do nothing but mischief at this time. "If Governor Pickens had simply asked the President for an assurance that Fort Sumter should not be occupied," wrote Trescot somewhat later, "and that Anderson should be so instructed, I think it could have been obtained." But the Governor's outright demand, if persisted in, would have released the President from his pledge to maintain the *status quo* in Charleston Harbor. Besides, the South Carolina Convention was deliberating on the Ordinance of Secession; it was imperative to avoid any open issues until

the state could send properly authorized commissioners
to present the Ordinance of Secession and to negotiate
with the Federal Government. A joint telegram was
sent to Pickens advising that he withdraw his letter,
and on this occasion the Governor accepted the counsel of cooler heads.

The convention had had its consummating session at
Institute Hall in Charleston on the afternoon of December 20. The Ordinance of Secession was adopted
without debate in forty-five minutes by a vote of 208
to 89. In the jubilation of the moment several delegates started a row over posssession of the historic
pen with which the ordinance had been signed. The
dense crowd of delegates and spectators swarmed to
the two palmetto trees which flanked the president's
chair and stripped them bare for souvenirs.

A messenger with a copy of the ordinance galloped
to the camp of Colonel Pettigrew's First Regiment of
South Carolina Rifles, where it was read to the men
amid shouts and cheers. Fifteen minutes after the ordinance had been adopted the Charleston *Mercury*
was on the streets with an extra: "THE UNION IS
DISSOLVED!" Wild excitement followed the news as
it spread through the city. All business was suspended,
and the music of the military bands was nearly
drowned out by the fierce enthusiasm of a people in
rebellion. Nearly every hat sported a cockade, and
palmetto flags and bunting of all colors were displayed
on every building. Throughout the business district,
merchants and tradespeople, even Northern business-
men, caught the popular fever and displayed crude
posters foretelling the glorious future of the state.

St. Michael's chimes rang out "Auld Lang Syne"

to the accompaniment of all the city's church bells.
At the post office someone fired a cannon. Even the
sun came out after three days of rainy weather. South
Carolina, for better or for worse, was now absolutely
committed. Four days later Pickens proclaimed South
Carolina "a free and independent nation."

On December 23 Anderson received new orders
from Secretary of War Floyd:

> It is neither expected nor desired that you
> should expose your own life or that of your men
> in a hopeless conflict in defense of these forts. If
> they are invested or attacked by a force so su-
> perior that resistance would, in your judgment, be
> a useless waste of life, it will be your duty to yield
> to necessity and make the best terms in your
> power. This will be the conduct of an honorable,
> brave and humane officer, and you will be fully
> justified in such action. *These orders are strictly
> confidential and not to be communicated even to
> the officers under your command without close
> necessity.*

The guns of Moultrie pointed harmlessly out to
sea; the attack on the fort—and one now seemed inevitable—would come from the land, directed at the
unguarded rear. Anderson was powerless and isolated.
He had received from Washington neither reinforcements nor the authorization to withdraw to a stronger
position. There was no Federal policy; the only official voice which Anderson heard was that of Floyd.
The Secretary of War's orders (which Anderson did
not divulge to his officers until April) now thrust home
to him the necessity for an immediate decision. The

best he could hope for in Moultrie, where he felt
threatened by an attack which might be launched at
any moment, was a quick struggle and an acceptable
surrender.

"Forts constructed in an enemy's country, and left
unguarded, are built for the enemy," Anderson's
second-in-command, Captain Abner Doubleday observed some years after. Certain that Anderson would
stay at Moultrie, Floyd allowed Sumter to be repaired
and armed—for future use by the rebels. Unless Anderson were to seize the initiative and take over Sumter, he and his garrison were destined to be the vic-
tims of a quickening struggle between a reluctant
Union and the aggressive state which had recently
been a part of it. But he would have to disobey Floyd.

CHAPTER
FIVE

"Anderson has opened the ball"

It had rained all Christmas night. The morning of December 26 dawned pale but clear. The usual sounds of the men getting up in the barracks at Moultrie floated out over the harbor and mingled with the cries of gulls circling the fort. The rising sun quickened highlights on the monstrous bronze cannon under which workmen would soon be going about their repairs.

Looking out over the parapets, the men at Moultrie could see the giant form of Sumter a little over a mile away, as she rose out of the dawn's mist fifty forbidding feet into the winter air. At 6:30 soldiers and laborers got to work at Moultrie, their established routine broken only by Anderson's orders that the fort's hospital be moved inside the walls from its temporary site outside. Anderson instructed Captain Foster to make sure that all the fort's boats were in good condition and could be available by that evening. In doing so, Foster was to avoid all contact with the Southern guard boats patrolling the channel, one of which, Anderson bitterly recognized, was named after his father-in-law, General Duncan Lamont Clinch.

Anderson worked quickly and quietly. He sent for Lieutenant Norman J. Hall and told the young officer to ready three schooners: "Take the women and children and six months' supply of provisions to Fort Johnson. If you are questioned by Secessionist patrols, tell them we are sending off the families of the officers to the North because they are in the way." Anderson instructed Hall to sail the schooners to Fort Johnson, make a pretense of inspecting the barracks to select proper quarters, but not to let the passengers and stores land. He was to delay at Fort Johnson until he heard two guns being fired and then sail boats and cargoes as quickly as possible to Fort Sumter.

A little later that morning the schooners drew into the wharf to pick up the garrison's forty-five women and children. Lieutenant Hall started to load them and by noon everything was in readiness for their departure. As the schooners prepared to leave, two men from Charleston, who had been watching the loading, started to interrogate Hall. Where were they going? Why? What was that box marked "One Thousand Ball Cartridges" doing on board? Hall managed to satisfy the men and removed the objectionable box, which, he realized, had been put there by mistake. The Southerners departed peacefully for Charleston.

While Hall was carrying out his orders, Lieutenants Snyder and Meade of the Engineers were busy following Foster's instructions to supervise the removal of the fort's garrison of seven officers and 65

HARPER'S WEEKLY.

A JOURNAL OF CIVILIZATION.

Vol. V.—No. 227.]   NEW YORK, SATURDAY, MAY 4, 1861.   [SINGLE COPIES SIX CENTS.
$2 50 PER YEAR IN ADVANCE.

Entered according to Act of Congress, in the Year 1861, by Harper & Brothers, in the Clerk's Office of the District Court for the Southern District of New York.

The house tops in Charleston during the bombardment of Sumter

Major Robert Anderson, photographed at Fort Sumter in February 1861 by George Cook of Charleston

President James Buchanan and his Cabinet. Standing (left to right): Lewis Cass, President Buchanan, Howell Cobb, Judge Joseph Holt. Seated: Jacob Thompson, John B. Floyd, Isaac Toucey, Jeremiah Black

Major Robert Anderson and his officers at Fort Sumter, February 1861. Standing (left to right): Captain Truman Seymour, Lieutenant G. W. Snyder, Lieutenant Jeff C. Davis, Lieutenant R. K. Meade. Seated: Captain Abner Doubleday, Major Anderson, Assistant Surgeon Samuel Wylie Crawford, Captain J. G. Foster

ABOVE LEFT: John B. Floyd, U. S. Secretary of War,
1857-1860

ABOVE RIGHT: Francis W. Pickens, Governor of
South Carolina, 1860-1862

ABOVE LEFT: Lieutenant General Winfield Scott.
Daguerreotype by Mathew B. Brady

ABOVE RIGHT: General Pierre Gustave Toutant
Beauregard

The Confederate floating battery during the bombardment of Fort Sumter. From *Harper's Weekly*

The first gun fired for the Union from Fort Sumter. Engraving from a drawing made in consultation with Abner Doubleday

Interior of Fort Sumter after the bombardment in April 1861.
On the left are the burned-out barracks; on the right are the
flagstones taken up from the parade ground as a precaution against
shell splinters. *Engraved from a contemporary drawing*

Exterior of Fort Sumter after it was evacuated in April 1861

The flag-raising ceremony at Fort Sumter, April 14, 1865. On the parapet the gun crews are waiting to fire the salute. Major Anderson, Henry Ward Beecher, and other dignitaries are seated on the platform under the flag-draped arches

The deserted fort after the ceremonies. The walls have been reduced to rubble by the years of bombardment

enlisted men from Moultrie to Sumter. They had pro-
cured three six-oared barges and two four-oared boats,
belonging to the Engineer Department, which lay hidden under the sea wall on the beach below the fort.

In order to cover his true intent, Anderson had
work on the landside defenses continued throughout
the day. Surgeon Samuel Crawford was one of the
first men to get an inkling of what Anderson was up
to when he discovered, on a visit to Sumter, that all
Sumter's boats were gone. "Crawford," an officer
there said to him, "go back to Moultrie and don't
take your eyes off Anderson." Crawford returned to
Moultrie; he found Anderson standing by the parapet,
looking toward the open sea. At that moment a large
steamer of the Savannah line, heading north, slowed
up and changed her course as if to enter the harbor.
Anderson turned to Crawford, saying, "I hope she
will not attempt to come in. It would greatly em-
barrass me. I intend to move to Fort Sumter tonight." He swore the doctor to secrecy. Crawford
was concerned about his hospital; Anderson assured
him that it would be safe at Moultrie until the next
morning.

As dusk began to settle over Moultrie and Sumter,
deckhands aboard the Southern patrol boats trimmed
the wicks and lighted their running lights. There was
time for amenities. Mrs. Abner Doubleday, one of the
last women left at the fort, sent her husband to in-
vite Anderson to take tea with them. Anderson's
second-in-command, Doubleday had more than twenty
years before left behind him the crude baseball dia-
mond at Cooperstown, New York, for West Point
and an Army career. Now he had come to a turning
point. When he reached Anderson and the group of

tense and anxious officers with him, he was unprepared
for the major's orders: "Captain, in twenty minutes
you will leave this fort with your company for Fort
Sumter." Doubleday moved fast, strangely relieved by
Anderson's decision, and with little inclination to give
more than a passing worry to the effect of this move
on the Southerners. He remembered that a month
before he had suggested to Anderson that the move
to Sumter might be advisable. Anderson quickly dismissed the idea. "The North does not believe there is
going to be a war," he had said. "My orders are to remain in Moultrie." Doubleday had not ventured to
pursue the subject further.

Now he ordered out his men, saw to it they were
properly equipped. He rushed to his quarters, told his
wife to pack, and while she was throwing her clothes
into her trunk he warned her to hurry. "The fighting
may begin at any moment!" he said. With the help
of two of his men Captain Doubleday got his wife
and her belongings to the main gate, where the two
said an anxious farewell. He strapped on his revolver, tied a blanket across his shoulders, and reported
at the sally port to Major Anderson that his men
were ready to leave.

At this announcement Captain Foster, in command
of the rear guard, with Lieutenant Jeff C. Davis,
Surgeon Crawford, two sergeants and three enlisted
men, made for the sea battery, where they took up
stations at five loaded columbiads. They would cover
the men on their short but perilous trip by boat to
Sumter. Major Anderson gave his final instructions.
"Captain Foster," he said quietly, "if there is any
attempt to interfere with the passage of the boats

upon the part of the guard boat, you are to fire on her."

Doubleday, Anderson and Captain Truman Seymour, cautioning the men to be silent, slipped out of the sally port and marched the quarter of a mile down the road to Moultrieville which was fortunately almost empty; the Charleston militia was nowhere in sight and the village seemed deserted. In a few minutes the men reached the sea wall, where Doubleday met with Lieutenants Meade and Snyder, as arranged. Snyder pointed to the boats intended for Doubleday's men, saying, "Captain, those boats are for your men. I am starting with my party up the coast." Silently the men climbed aboard. Lieutenant Snyder, in the lead boat with Major Anderson, who personally carried the garrison's flag, waited until Meade and his men were safely in the second boat, and then cast off his painter. Doubleday followed. The boats swung into the channel and as a precaution headed on different courses for Sumter.

Snyder's party began rowing in Moultrie's direction and narrowly escaped detection by a guard boat patrolling inshore. Doubleday's men, inexperienced at rowing, were nearing the middle of the channel when a guard boat bore down on them, the noise of its paddle wheels growing louder. The twilight had partially cloaked their tangled efforts to keep the oars in unison, but not sufficiently. Doubleday whipped off his cap with its bright braid and ordered his men to hurry out of their coats, the shiny buttons of which gleamed in the nearing lights of the patrol boat. The boat stopped its paddle wheels, slowly drifted by, and, apparently satisfied that this was not a military party, moved on. Saved by the semi-disguise, Doubleday and his men swiftly accomplished the rest of their journey and were the first to reach Fort Sumter.

They made the landing and advanced in combat formation through the main gate, where they were met by a gang of civilian workmen. To make sure that the workmen, some of whom were Southern sympathizers, would not resist, Doubleday placed his men as guards inside and outside the main gate and on the ramparts, their rifles on the ready. So far all had gone with phenomenal smoothness. The fort was secured for Anderson's men, and Doubleday now sent the boats back to Moultrie for the remainder of the troops. Surgeon Crawford, from a lookout spot on the ramparts, watched the boats cross and recross, counting three trips in all as the last barge with a cargo of bedding tied up at the Sumter wharf. Anderson now ordered two signal guns fired. Lieutenant Hall, at Fort Johnson with the women and children, heard the reports, acknowledged the all-clear, and started his schooners toward Sumter.

By eight o'clock Anderson's entire command, with the exception of the rear guard at Moultrie, was safely inside Sumter's great walls. Surgeon Crawford, returning from Sumter in order to collect his hospital supplies, arrived at Moultrie in time to help Foster and his men in their work of precautionary destruction. They spiked every gun of the entire battery facing Sumter and rendered them temporarily useless. The doctor helped push five big guns from their carriages to the parapet below. The men chopped up the wooden gun carriages, set them on fire, and toppled the flagstaff into a ditch. This work done, they managed to get a vital supply of small arms and all the hospital supplies transferred to Sumter, but they were forced to abandon a month's provisions, the garrison's entire store of fuel oil, and some personal effects. They destroyed a good part of the ammunition they could not take with them.

When it was all over, the Southern patrol boat *Nina,* with a detachment of the Washington Light Infantry aboard, dropped anchor in the stream between the forts, long after its customary hour for doing so, and there spent the night, her captain utterly unaware of what had taken place.

When Major Anderson was certain that his men and equipment were safe at Sumter, he retired to his new quarters and sat down to write two letters. The first was to Elizabeth, his wife. "Thanks be to God," he wrote her. "I give them with my whole heart for His having given me the will, and shown me the way to take my command to this fort. I can now breathe freely. The whole force of South Carolina would not venture to attack us. Our crossing was accomplished between six and eight o'clock. I am satisfied that there was no suspicion of what we were going to do. I have no doubt that the news of what I have done will be telegraphed to New York this night."

The second missive was a direct and impersonal report to Colonel Cooper of the Adjutant General's office in Washington: "I have the honor to report that I have just completed, by the blessing of God, the removal to this fort of all my garrison. We have one year's supply of hospital stores and about four months' supply of provisions for my command." Anderson concluded: "This step I have taken was, in my opinion, necessary to prevent the effusion of blood." When he had finished his correspondence, Anderson made a last inspection of the guards and lookouts before he retired for the night.

December 27 was a fine, bright day. As the soldiers on the walls of Sumter waited patiently for their relief to come from below, they saw the boat *Nina* pull up her anchor and come steaming toward the fort. The *Nina* slowed her engine as she neared the walls and went drifting by, giving her amazed crew a good and shocking look at Anderson's men lining the parapets. The *Nina* quickly swung around in the channel and steamed at full speed to her wharf in Charleston. Her crew jumped ashore and spread the alarm, rousing Charleston's people, who reacted with panic and anger. Before much of the morning had passed, the city was in an uproar. Fearing a Federal bombardment, Charleston bankers suspended specie payment; Anderson was denounced as a traitor.

Mary Boykin Chesnut, in her Charleston home, was visited by a friend, Mrs. Gidiere, who told her breathlessly, "Mary, Major Anderson has moved into Fort Sumter, while Governor Pickens slept serenely." Mrs. Chesnut's immediate reaction was rather self-consciously historical, but her thoughts provide a stylish and perhaps typical response to what was still regarded in many places as a romantic encounter: "The row is fast and furious now," she wrote. "Anderson has united the Cotton States. Now for Virginia. Anderson has opened the ball! Those who want a row are in high glee. Those who dread it are glum and thoughtful enough. The talk is: Fort Sumter must be taken; and it is one of the strongest forts!"

The official reaction was to demand from Anderson

his reasons for moving to Sumter. Accordingly, Governor Pickens sent his aide-de-camp, Colonel Pettigrew, to Fort Sumter that morning to get an explanation. When Pettigrew and Major Ellison Capers reached the fort, they were shown at once to Anderson's quarters. The meeting was stiffly formal: Pettigrew and Capers refused to be seated. Pettigrew, impatient to get on with it, asked Anderson if he could talk in front of the Federal officers who were in the room with them. "Certainly, sir," replied Anderson. "These are all my officers; I have no secrets from them."

Pettigrew came right to the point. Governor Pickens, he said, was quite surprised when he discovered that Anderson had reinforced Sumter. "I have not reinforced the fort. I have simply moved my command here," Anderson declared; he was, after all, responsible for every fort in the harbor and could garrison whichever he deemed best. Colonel Pettigrew disagreed. Governor Pickens, he assured Anderson, was led to believe, when he assumed office, that President Buchanan had pledged that all property within the limits of the state was to remain as it was; that no reinforcements would be sent in, and that this applied especially to Fort Sumter. It was also understood that, on the one hand, South Carolina would not damage any Federal property in the harbor, and on the other, the status of the forts would remain unchanged. Governor Pickens, Pettigrew reported, was troubled by matters which "greatly complicated" the situation; in fact, "bloodshed might now be avoided no longer."

Anderson maintained his composure. He had not, he answered calmly, been informed of any such pledge

on the part of Buchanan. Furthermore, his position
had been threatened nightly by South Carolina troops.

Major Capers, who, up to this point, had been silent, burst out "How?" "By sending out steamers
armed and carrying troops," Anderson flung back.
"These steamers," he continued, "passed the fort
going north," where troops could easily be landed. If
one hundred riflemen occupied the sandhills near
Moultrie, his own troops could not man their guns.
"Any man with a military head must see this." Anderson claimed that he avoided this danger by moving the garrison, "my sole object being to prevent
bloodshed." Capers denied that an attack on Fort
Moultrie had ever been contemplated by South Carolina troops and declared that the boats patrolled the
harbor as much to prevent disorder among Charleston's citizens as for any other reason. Anderson said
he frankly doubted this and, as he was not clairvoy-
ant, had no way of knowing what the state's intentions were when they sent the boats out into the harbor at night.

Then, with characteristic openness, Anderson said,
"In this controversy between the North and South,
my sympathies are entirely with the South! These gentlemen—" he pointed to his own officers—"know it
perfectly well."

But his duty, he added, was solely to the Federal
Government and he would do it, regardless of personal
sentiments.

"Well, sir, however that may be," said Colonel
Pettigrew, "the Governor of the State directs me to
say to you, return to Fort Moultrie."

"Make my compliments to the Governor and say
to him that I decline to accede to his request; I can-

not and will not go back!" Anderson said. The two officers bowed, and were gone.

When Pettigrew reported to Pickens on his meeting with Anderson, Pickens gave him immediate orders to seize and occupy the forts in the harbor and the arsenal in the city. "You are to take possession of Castle Pinckney. You are to act with the greatest discretion and prudence, and to let it be known that you take possession in the name of the Governor of South Carolina, and in consequence of the extraordinary orders executed last night in relation to Fort Moultrie, and with a view at present to prevent further destruction of public propery, and as a measure of safety also."

Identical orders were issued to Lieutenant Colonel W. G. De Saussure, First Regiment of Artillery, who was instructed to occupy Fort Moultrie and Sullivan's Island.

Just before noon, Major Anderson on Sumter was conducting a thanksgiving ceremony on the parade ground, his entire command of soldiers, workmen, and military band in attendance. The Reverend Mathias Harris, Fort Chaplain, offered up thanks for the garrison's safe arrival and prayed that the United States emblem would once again float over the entire nation in peace. Major Anderson, who had been on his knees, arose and hauled the flag to the head of the flagstaff.

At two o'clock in the afternoon Colonel Pettigrew, with two companies of his rifle regiment, the Washington Light Infantry and Meagher's Guards, marched to a Charleston wharf, boarded the *Nina,* and headed for Castle Pinckney. The men under him were eager for action.

The only occupants of the fort were Lieutenant
R. K. Meade (a loyal officer later compelled by family
ties and pressures to go over to the Southern side), the
gang of workmen, and the old sergeant and his family. When the Southern soldiers approached, the workmen started to disperse, and Meade had to order them
to their quarters. Pettigrew led his men up to the main
gate, assigning some of them to cover the parapets
with their rifles, and demanded entrance. Meade refused, but when he saw Pettigrew's men set up scal-
ing ladders, he realized that resistance was futile and
allowed the gate to be opened. Making the capture
of Pinckney formal, Pettigrew drew a paper from his
pocket and read it aloud to Meade. Its contents authorized Pettigrew to occupy the fort in the name of
the Governor of South Carolina. Meade interrupted
the reading. He did not and could not recognize the
Governor's authority, he said, but since resistance was
out of the question he wanted to register his protest
to the occupation. Pettigrew tried to force Meade to
accept receipts for the fort and its property, but
Meade would not recognize Pettigrew's and Pickens'
authority even this far. During the discussion the
Southern soldiers formed ranks on the parade ground.

"You are free to leave the fort, sir," Pettigrew
told Meade, "but once you leave I cannot allow you
to return." There was little point to Meade's remaining at Pinckney. After being assured that the
sergeant and his family would be treated well, he left
for Sumter to report the incident to Anderson, who
had had his field glasses trained on Pinckney all the
while. Doubleday, who had been standing beside the
major, reported later that Anderson vented his anger
in expressions that could not be decently repeated.

Almost simultaneous with the capture of Pinckney, Colonel De Saussure, with two hundred picked men of the First Regiment of Artillery, crossed to Sullivan's Island. He believed rumors that the entire area had been mined and so he led his men cautiously through the main streets of the reservation. He had only to subdue a single occupant of the fort, an overseer left there by the engineers. The next morning Fort Moultrie was permanently occupied by state troops. Despite the efforts of Anderson's rear guard, the Secessionists found themselves richer by 56 light and heavy guns in good condition, columbiads, mortars, and some ammunition, in addition to the spiked guns which could be repaired. In a single day, December 27, Fort Moultrie, Castle Pinckney, the U. S. Arsenal and Customs House in Charleston had been seized and the palmetto flag raised over them—and not one drop of blood had been spilled.

On December 28 the New York *Herald*, in its morning edition, headlined the news from Charleston:

MAJOR ANDERSON ABANDONS FORT MOULTRIE AND SPIKES THE GUNS! GREAT EXCITEMENT IN CHARLESTON! CONVENTION IN SECRET SESSION! STATE MILITIA ORDERED OUT! MAJOR ANDERSON DISOBEYS ORDERS!

Major Anderson, who commands Fort Moultrie, knowing the position to be untenable, evacuated it and took possession of Fort Sumter, an almost impregnable post where, in the event of an attack upon United States property, he would be able to defend it against great odds. It is conceded that it would require a continuous bombardment of six months with guns of the heaviest metal to destroy Fort Sumter, and then it could only be

done, if at all, by chipping off the masonry piece
by piece. Sumter is the strongest fort of its size in
the world, and could only be taken by starving
out the garrison.

The Charleston *Courier* had this reaction:

Major Anderson has achieved the unenviable
distinction of opening civil war between American
citizens, by an act of gross breach of faith. He has
grossly violated a solemn pledge given by his
Chief and accepted by South Carolina, that he had
all possible assurances that his honor, position,
and duty would be respected until a proper and
open declaration of war.

CHAPTER
SIX

"He still commands the harbor"

On the morning of December 27, while Anderson was beginning the backbreaking task of putting Sumter in fighting order, the commissioners appointed by the South Carolina Secession Convention prepared for an interview with President Buchanan. They were instructed by Pickens to present the Ordinance of Secession and negotiate for the evacuation of the forts in Charleston Harbor.

At their rented mansion on Franklin Row, the commissioners—R. W. Barnwell, J. H. Adams, and James L. Orr—were conferring with Trescot when Colonel Wigfall, the senator from Texas, burst into the room. "Major Anderson has abandoned Fort Moultrie, destroyed the armament, cut down the flagstaff, and removed his command to Fort Sumter!"

Trescot was the first to recover from the shock. "Well, at any rate, Colonel," he said to Wigfall, "true or not, I pledge my life, if it has been done, it has been done without orders from Washington."

At this moment John B. Floyd joined the group. The Secretary of War of the United States had voluntarily come to a house where a group of men, dedicated to the establishment of their own separate government, were plotting their tactics. He had not invited the commissioners to come to his office, nor had he steered clear of them for fear of compromising himself: he was with them in spirit and in body.

Trescot turned to him: "Colonel Wigfall has just brought us this news, and as you were coming up the stairs I said I would pledge my life it was without orders."

"You can do no more," Floyd answered. "You can pledge your life, Mr. Trescot, that it is not so. It is impossible. It would be not only without orders," he continued, his voice rising, "but in the face of orders." Floyd studied the faces of the men around him. "To be very frank," he said with deliberation, "Anderson was instructed in case he had to abandon his position to dismantle Fort Sumter, not Fort Moultrie."

"I am afraid, Governor, it is too true," Trescot said after a pause. Two telegrams confirming Wigfall's report had arrived from Charleston.

Trescot and the commissioners, joined by Senator Jefferson Davis of Mississippi and Senator R. M. T. Hunter of Virginia, drove that morning to the White House and were ushered into the President's study. When he entered the room, Buchanan embarked on the small talk with which men customarily open a diplomatic encounter—a trivial remark to Senator Hunter about the removal of the consul at Liverpool.

Hunter, nervous and impatient, made no reply, and it was Jefferson Davis who stated their mission. "Mr. President," he said, "we have called upon an infinitely graver matter than any consulate. Have you received any intelligence from Charleston in the last few hours?"

"None," replied Buchanan.

"Then I have a great calamity to announce to you," Davis said, reporting the news of Anderson's move to Sumter. "You are surrounded with dishonor on all sides."

Buchanan, who had been leaning against the mantelpiece, crushed out his cigar and lowered himself heavily into a chair. "My God! Are the calamities never to come singularly? I call God to witness: You gentlemen, better than anybody, *know* that this is not only without but against my orders. It is against my policy!" The President was still skeptical of the report—"I think it strange that the War Department has not heard of it"—and summoned Floyd, who read aloud a telegram he had just sent to Anderson: "There is a report here that you have abandoned Fort Moultrie, burned your carriages, and gone to Fort Sumter. It is not believed, as you had no orders to justify it. Say at once what could have given rise to such a story."

Proceeding on the assumption that the report of Anderson's move was accurate, Buchanan and the commissioners began an urgent and troubling discussion. The President must take immediate action, the commissioners urged, for it was probable that South Carolina would now seize and garrison the remaining forts and the arsenal and would launch an attack on Fort Sumter. If Buchanan would support his Decem-

ber 10 pledge to maintain the *status quo* in Charleston
Harbor and would order Anderson back to Moultrie,
there might still be a chance of averting a collision.

The commissioners pleaded and threatened. At first
Buchanan seemed disposed to order Anderson to return his garrison to Moultrie, and then he hesitated: "I cannot condemn Major Anderson unheard."
No one asked that he condemn Anderson, the commissioners told him. All that they wanted from him
was a statement that, if Anderson had moved to Sumter for reasons other than an actual or threatened attack on Moultrie, Buchanan would order him back.
If they could receive this assurance, then Buchanan
could have the necessary time to consult with his
Cabinet.

Buchanan refused to give this assurance and, obviously shaken by the swift movement of events, adjourned the meeting. The prospect before him was ap-
palling. The news on this one day had shattered his
hopes of confining secession to South Carolina alone.
It was now likely that Anderson's move, if verified,
would arouse the Cotton and Border States into join-
ing South Carolina and that compromise measures still
pending in the Senate would be either suspended or
defeated.

The next four days were to be a series of debates
and consultations, demands and *démarches*. The South
Carolina commissioners renewed their demands for
Anderson's withdrawal, reminded Buchanan again and
again of his pledge, and added threats of war. "This
is a grave question," the President could only reply.
"You are pressing me too importunately. You must
give me time to say my prayers." During this time
Buchanan called a series of critical Cabinet meetings,

meetings at which the Government's divided policy and factional bitterness became tragically apparent.

By the afternoon of December 27 Secretary of War Floyd received his answer from Major Anderson: "The telegram is correct. I abandoned Fort Moultrie because I was certain that if attacked my men must have been sacrificed, and the command of the harbor lost. I spiked the guns and destroyed the carriages to keep the guns from being used against us. If attacked, the garrision would never have surrendered without a fight."

On his way in to the Cabinet meeting Buchanan had called, Floyd summoned Major Buell and ordered him to stand by in the event that his direct knowledge of Anderson's position and of Floyd's "verbal" orders would be of use. "This is a very unfortunate move of Major Anderson's," Floyd told him as they stood outside the Cabinet room. "It has made war inevitable."

Surprised, Buell replied, "I do not think so, sir. On the contrary, I think that it will tend to avert war, if war can be averted."

"But it has compromised the President!" Floyd said. As the doors to the Cabinet room were opened, Floyd left to take his place at the long table.

The meeting was stormy. Floyd took the lead in denouncing Anderson. There was no reason for Anderson's move to Sumter, he shouted. Anderson had disobeyed orders. He had acted without authority and had broken an established agreement. It was at this point that Secretary of State Jeremiah H. Black, who had replaced General Lewis Cass and Cass's stand-in Trescot only a few days before, interrupted the tirade. He cited Floyd's instructions conveyed by Buell

to Anderson, carefully committed to paper and filed
with the War Department. Anderson had *not* disobeyed orders, Black declared; on the contrary, he had
acted wholly in accordance with his orders to move
his command into any fort that he chose if he had
evidence of an impending attack. The paper was
produced and read to the President and the Cabinet,
and Black added to its impact by pointing out that
the paper had been endorsed by both Floyd ("This
is in conformity to my instructions to Major Buell")
and by Buchanan. The President later recalled that
he had signed the paper as a routine document, never
having actually read it or even remembered its existence. Black's angry move was a bombshell; both Buchanan and Floyd were embarrassed, and the meeting
adjourned in confusion.

Buchanan could still take some comfort from Anderson's act. So far, the move to Sumter had had no
direct results except threats and raised voices on the
part of the commissioners. If the commissioners believed that Sumter was a strong and strategic fort,
they would not propose an attack. And if Anderson's
move turned out to be a temporary deterrent to war,
why then not leave things as they were? But Buchanan still had to answer the commissioners and, in
his own eyes and in theirs, find justification for
what seemed a broken pledge.

It was Black who rescued the President from his
dilemma. Unwilling to accept the personal pledge of
Buchanan as being binding on the Government, Black,
after a Cabinet meeting on the 28th, threatened to
resign unless the President took a firm stand with the
commissioners. "Do you, too, talk of leaving me?"
the weary and baffled Buchanan asked with some

feeling. "You do not seem to appreciate," he added, "that my personal honor as a gentleman is involved." Black, his dignity and firmness carrying great conviction, replied that the President must retire from any agreement that would tie his hands in the execution of the law of the land, that no personal pledge was valid in the circumstances.

Buchanan gave in. He gave Black full authority to draft recommendations for a reply to the commissioners. Black retired to Attorney General Stanton's office and sat down to write. As he finished a page Stanton copied it in his own hand and sent the original to Buchanan. The recommendations were firm and positive, the first statement of a definite Federal policy. South Carolina had no right to be represented by diplomatic officers, Black declared, and it was entirely wrong for the United States to enter into negotiations over its own property in Charleston Harbor. Sumter should not only be held but also powerfully maintained, if not for combat, then to control the harbor and execute the revenue laws. Major Anderson, continued Black's paper, was "a gallant and meritorious officer, who is entitled to a fair hearing before he is condemned: he has saved the country, I solemnly believe, when its day was darkest and its peril most extreme. He has done everything that mortal man could do to repair the fatal error which the Administration has committed in not sending down enough troops to hold the forts. He has kept the strongest one. He still commands the harbor."

Black recommended specific action. The warships *Brooklyn* and *Macedonian* should be sent to Charleston immediately. A messenger should be sent to Anderson to let him know that his Government would

not desert him. Troops from New York, or from
Fortress Monroe in Virginia, should be sent to reinforce Sumter. "If this be done," Black concluded,
"all may yet be, not well, but comparatively safe.
If not, I can see nothing before us but disaster and
ruin to the country."

On the evening of December 29, fortified by
Black's counsel, Buchanan called another meeting of
his divided Cabinet; he read to them his proposed reply to the South Carolina commissioners. Present
were Black, Secretary of the Treasury Philip Thomas,
Secretary of the Interior Jacob Thompson, Postmaster General Joseph Holt, Secretary of the Navy Isaac
Toucey, Attorney General Edwin M. Stanton, and
Secretary of War John B. Floyd. It was a critical
and uncomfortable confrontation.

Despite the delaying actions of Floyd and Thompson, Buchanan managed to read through his reply to
its firm conclusion: "I am urged immediately to withdraw the troops from the harbor of Charleston, and
am informed that without this negotiation is impossible. This I cannot do. This I will not do!"

A flushed and angry Floyd interrupted the discussion that followed. He jumped from his chair, waved
a sheet of paper, and read a statement he had prepared before the meeting: "I deeply regret to feel
myself under the necessity of tendering my resignation
as Secretary of War, because I can no longer hold
office under my convictions of patriotism nor with
honor, subjected, as I am, to a violation of solemn
pledges and plighted faith."

Floyd's resignation was only one of the effects of
the new policy of purpose and vigor that Black im-
posed on Buchanan. On December 31 the now

steadfast President read his reply to the commissioners and reiterated his refusal to withdraw Anderson from Sumter. They realized the radical change in Buchanan and left the meeting with little hope for a peaceful negotiation. The North could no longer be compromised, it seemed. Yet one final attempt was made.

On Trescot's urging, Senator Hunter later that day called on Buchanan with a new proposal: if Anderson were withdrawn from Sumter to Moultrie, South Carolina would withdraw her forces from the other forts and would guarantee that Anderson would be as safe in Moultrie as he would be in Washington. Hunter soon returned from his interview. "Tell the commissioners it is hopeless," he said to Trescot. "The President has taken his ground. I can't repeat what passed, but if you can get a telegram to Charleston, telegraph at once to your people to sink vessels in the channel of the harbor." Trescot wrote out the message, and, to avoid detection, sent it by courier to Richmond, from where it was telegraphed on. A new phase of the drama was beginning: the relief of Sumter must be prevented.

In this crisis, Buchanan's Cabinet was disintegrating. Lewis Cass and Howell Cobb, now replaced by Thomas, had already left; Thomas himself was soon to go south along with Thompson. And Floyd was out, in Virginia, openly working for the Secessionist cause. When questioned about his Secretary of War's sudden resignation, Buchanan gave out the story that he himself had requested it on December 23 on account of an apparent shortage of $870,000 worth of Indian Trust Bonds which, it was alleged, Floyd had feloniously withdrawn from the Department of the Interior. Not long after he left Washington, a grand jury charged Floyd with "maladministration in office, complicity in the abstraction of the bonds, and conspiracy against the Government." Buchanan also discovered that Floyd had, without authorization, been transferring muskets and rifles from Northern to Southern arsenals.

Thus, when it was almost too late, Buchanan came around to recognizing the comparative values and loyalties of Major Anderson and Secretary Floyd. Both Buchanan and Anderson had Secretary of State Black, more than any other man in the Government, to be thankful to. The Major was now secure in his fort, one of the military prizes of the entire coast. He would remain there for 103 days.

CHAPTER
SEVEN

"Like a sheep tied watching the butcher"

Aroused by the failure of his commission in Washington, Governor Pickens now labeled Anderson "enemy" and declared Fort Sumter to be a menace to the city and to the state itself. He determined that Anderson should not remain secure in his command of the harbor and he ordered the systematic construction of a war machine designed specifically to drive out the small Federal garrison. This machine consisted of the forts and installations in Charleston Harbor.

From the ramparts of Sumter, Anderson and his men watched in dismay as Southern workmen and soldiers went about building up the batteries which faced them across the harbor. Anderson's own strategy, though it had brought him to a stronger position, tied his hands. The harbor was closed, and no reinforcements could reach him except under armed escort. All supplies and provisions from Charleston were cut off

from him by Pickens' orders. Only mail was allowed
to reach the men at the fort. As he watched the ring
of forts around him grow more deadly day by day,
Anderson admitted to one of his officers, "I feel like
a sheep tied watching the butcher sharpening his
knife." But the morale of the garrison remained high,
and the major felt that Sumter could do creditably
well against any force Pickens could muster—an opinion shared by his enemies.

Anderson did not know that Pickens' orders to arm
and ready the harbor installations were motivated
chiefly by his fear that Anderson would attack the
city. And Pickens was equally unaware that Anderson had no intention of bombarding Charleston; his
move to Sumter was primarily defensive. "Nothing,"
Anderson said of his tactics, "will be better calcu-
lated to prevent bloodshed than our being found in
such an attitude that it would be madness and folly to
attack us." It was in this ambience of fear that men
on both sides worked hurriedly to arm themselves.

At Castle Pinckney two detachments of men were
readying the fort for immediate defense and undergoing training in the use of the big guns there; their
artillery instructors were two former West Pointers.
At Moultrie engineer officers and two hundred men
were building shields to protect the batteries from the
guns of Sumter. On the tip of Sullivan's Island a
new battery was being constructed to guard the harbor and to prevent reinforcements from reaching Sumter. To provide an escape route for the men there
temporary bridges, with boats as pontoons, were
thrown up to connect the island with the mainland. On
Morris Island a detachment of forty cadets from
The Citadel Military Academy began work on an-

other battery. And at Fort Johnson fifty men were stationed to guard that side of the harbor and to prevent all supplies except mail from reaching Sumter. With military thoroughness Governor Pickens ordered powerful calcium lights installed in bombproof shelters on Morris and Sullivan's islands and hulks loaded with wood towed to the harbor entrance; the calcium and the wood were to be lighted as a warning signal and for the benefit of the artillery, should any Federal ship attempt a night run to Sumter.

As the work progressed, Pickens decided to solicit a professional military appraisal of the strength of Charleston Harbor. General Simons, whom Pickens had assigned to this survey, returned with a report in which he was compelled to sacrifice diplomacy and etiqette to military candor.

The fortifications, he told Pickens, were not sufficently protected. Moultrie was wholly untenable and even in the most favorable circumstances would "fall to the enemy after a short and bloody contest." Gunfire from Sumter could immediately sever lines of communication between Moultrie and Johnson and sink the transport Pickens proposed to send to Morris Island with troops and supplies. The new Morris Island battery, Simons continued, was not ready and would not be ready by the time Pickens had set for its completion. And even if it were ready, the corps of cadets would not be able to handle the big guns, not one man among them having seen guns that size, much less manipulated them. The Federal ship *Harriet Lane* (named after Buchanan's niece), rumored to be on her way to Charleston, could easily steam past the battery at fourteen knots and probably land her troops at Sumter in fifteen minutes, even with the cadets firing at her. Should the ship bring Anderson two hundred and fifty regulars, commanded by experienced officers, Pickens' raw volunteer regiments would not stand a chance. The fortifications were poor, the men at them inadequately trained. "Why, then," Simons concluded, "all the preparation and expense if the work cannot but terminate in disastrous failure?"

Simons' objective report was not received with gratitude by Pickens, whose pride and ambitions as a military commander did not permit him to believe it. His Board of Ordnance offered him no consolation. On January 2, after considering Simons' report, they answered, "we concur generally." Pickens had to face facts. And yet he wrote, "The conclusions of that report I consider would be to order troops from Fort Moultrie and Sullivan's Island and Pinckney, and to abandon the attempt to keep our reinforcements, and in fact to yield without a struggle on every point, and thus break down the spirit of our people, and cover our cause with imbecility and probable ruin. I shall do no such thing, nor shall I hold any Council of War that may drive me to such conclusions!" He thus rationalized his military position by reverting to a moral and political one. He forged ahead, ignoring the warnings of men supposedly qualified to give them, and summoned his military engineers to draw up plans "for operating upon Fort Sumter, so as to reduce that fortress by batteries or other means."

The country's newspapers, meanwhile, had become aware of the drama and conflict in Charleston Harbor and were giving it all the space it deserved. A sympathetic public opinion, stimulated by a vote of confidence for Anderson in the House of Representatives, had transformed him into a hero overnight. "Touch not a hair of his head," declaimed a congressman from Ohio. "He is sacred today. He embodies the patriotism of millions!" *The New York Times* said that Anderson "has now become familiar as a household word." From all over the North letters poured into Washington demanding that troops and supplies be sent to him at once. Some letters submitted specific plans for coming to his aid. A Mr. James A. Hamilton of New York proposed that he escort a force of four hundred volunteers to Charleston, introduce them into Sumter as "guests" in civilian clothes, and leave them there as bona-fide soldiers under Anderson's command. The plan intrigued General Winfield Scott and he recommended it to Buchanan. But though Buchanan liked the idea, he denied the wisdom of reinforcing Anderson's garrison with volunteers; any call for volunteers, he felt, would be construed as an active preparation for war.

Buchanan, following the advice of Black, had been laying other plans. He sent secret orders to Captain David Farragut at Fortress Monroe in Virginia to hold the *U.S.S. Brooklyn* in readiness to proceed with a detachment of soldiers to Sumter. On December 29 Buchanan revealed these orders to Scott, who the next day instructed the commandant at Fortress Monroe to place 200 men from the garrison there aboard the *Brooklyn;* he was to do this as secretly as possible and to equip the men with twenty-five spare stand of arms and enough provisions for ninety days.

Scott was still not completely satisfied with the plan. He felt that a merchant steamer would be less likely to draw the enemy's fire than a warship. He discussed this idea with the Secretaries of War and the Navy and then with Buchanan. Since secrecy was more important than naval weapons in this case, Scott was able to convince the President that a less conspicuous, side-wheeled merchant steamer should be substituted for the *Brooklyn*. Moreover, Scott felt that Fortress Monroe, situated deep in "enemy" territory, should not be weakened by the withdrawal of 200 soldiers. He proposed that the men should instead come from the garrison at New York. Accordingly, he withdrew his orders to the Fortress Monroe commandant, but Farragut's *Brooklyn* was still to stand in readiness in case an armed escort vessel should be needed.

Scott had optimistically foreseen the President's agreement to this part of the plan; on December 27 he had spoken with a Mr. A. C. Schultze, a New York merchant on a business trip to Washington, about chartering a ship from him. Colonel Lorenzo Thomas now left Washington for New York, on Scott's orders, to examine Schultze's record and reliability and to satisfy himself that the New Yorker could provide the steamer with the necessary secrecy.

While Northern plans to relieve Anderson were crystallizing, spokesmen of patience and moderation in the South were being noisily outshouted by a public movement to seize Fort Sumter at any cost. "THE FORT MUST BE OURS!" screamed the headlines of the Charleston *Mercury*. In a fever of supercharged patriotism and emotion, Charlestonians came up with some ingenious and harebrained schemes for dislodging the major from his fort.

One man advocated that a group of stalwarts float down past the fort on a raft piled high with burning tar barrels and smoke the Yankees out "as you would a rabbit out of a hollow." Another suggested that a delegation of men go to the fort, each one carrying a concealed bomb of prussic acid, by which they would overcome the soldiers at close range. Another suggested the age-old remedy of bribery; just give each soldier ten dollars and a good talking to, and the garrison would hand over the fort without a fight—a nice peaceful solution.

All these schemes were published in the Charleston newspapers as letters to the editor. None was more romantically conceived than the plan for a floating battery, piled with cotton bales and heavily armed with cannon, to start down the channel past Sumter. Sharpshooters, hidden among the bales, would pick off the Federal soldiers as the battery floated by. Then, with Moultrie, Johnson and Pinckney backing them up with fire, a storming party, assisted by the fleet, could easily seize the fort. There were three flaws in this elaborate scheme: the forts were not ready to fire, there was no fleet, and, finally, Anderson's men could not be counted on to give up without a fight.

A plan that probably might have worked, and indeed was being followed by Pickens, was, as one letter writer put it, "the un-Christian mode of starving the men out by a protracted siege." Although the Governor was willing to make provision for the removal of women and children from Sumter, he allowed no commerce between the fort and the city except for the garrison's mail. Anderson was not permitted to buy fresh meats and vegetables, except surreptitiously and very intermittently.

On New Year's Day, Major Anderson received an unexpected and welcome visit from his wife. Pickens had given her permission to visit the fort accompanied by her brother, Bayard Clinch, Anderson's brother Larz, and the Charlestonian, Robert Gourdin. Anderson rushed to greet her at the sally port. Elizabeth gave Anderson news of their children and brought him up to date on the national crisis from which, though he was one of the central figures, he was curiously cut off. South Carolina, she told him, would soon be joined in secession by other states; the Confederacy grew in strength and purpose daily. She and Larz had some good news for him, however. He was told of a personal letter Larz had received from Buchanan. The President blamed the War Department for keeping him ignorant of official communications with Anderson; now that the situation was clarified everyone admired the masterly move to Sumter. The visit was brief. After a few hours Elizabeth and the small group returned to Charleston.

Anderson's official supporters went steadily ahead with their plan to send him the reinforcements and supplies he so desperately needed. On January 4 Colonel Thomas reported to General Scott that he was satisfied that Schultze could provide them with the necessary merchant ship. Arrangements were made for the steamship *Star of the West* to make the journey at a cost to the Government of $1,500 a day. The ship was to clear for New Orleans from New York without formal notice and as if for a routine trip; the troops were to be concealed below decks. In the interests of security all provisions were to be charged to the ship's account.

To prepare Major Anderson, a letter was to have been sent from Scott telling him that the *Star of the West* was on her way and explicitly stating that "should a fire likely to prove injurious be opened upon any vessel bringing reinforcements or supplies, or upon her boats, from any battery in the harbor, the guns of Fort Sumter may be employed to silence such fire, and the same in case of like fire upon Fort Sumter." It is one of the most baffling elements of the whole affair that either through negligence, accident or subversion, Anderson never received the letter. Ironically, on January 4, the day before the *Star of the West* left on her mission, a letter from Anderson was received in Washington; the major reported that he was secure at Sumter "where the Government could send additional troops at its leisure." This confident estimate of his situation was later to be the cause of confusion to the Government and embarrassment to Anderson.

During the day of preparation all military communication between New York and Washington was cut off. At five P.M. on the afternoon of January 5, the *Star of the West* slipped her cables from lower Manhattan and slowly steamed toward Governor's Island, where powder, shells and three months' supply of food for Anderson's garrison were loaded aboard.

Off Staten Island, a few minutes after seven o'clock, a small steamship, the *Lockwood,* drew near, was tied up to the *Star of the West,* and 200 officers and men carrying small arms and ammunition began to board. The transfer of the men to the *Star of the West* was accomplished as silently and quickly as possible; all lights were dimmed on the two ships as the men in gray overcoats and dark caps crossed the gangway. Such secrecy had been observed in planning the expedition that the two officers in command had been ignorant of their destination until a few hours before. The men under them were told only after they had boarded the *Star*. And then, according to the special correspondent of the New York *Evening Post* who also sailed on the *Star,* their prevailing questions were "Shall we get to Fort Sumter? If they attack us, who will protect us?" They were assured by their officers: "We fully expect the protection of Fort Sumter." At nine P.M., the *Star of the West* steamed off, crossed the bar, and headed south.

When Scott heard, on January 5, about the battery Pickens had had established on Morris Island, a battery whose guns would probably destroy any unarmed vessel entering the harbor, he was convinced that he was sending the *Star of the West* straight into a trap. He telegraphed New York to have the ship detained, but his orders arrived too late. The *Star of the West,* under her master, Captain McGowan, was already far out to sea, apparently only another merchant ship on a routine voyage south.

The ship could not be detained, but she could be protected. On January 7 Captain Farragut at Fortress Monroe was given orders for the *Brooklyn* to escort the *Star of the West;* he was to instruct Lieutenant Woods, when the two ships met, that if the landing at Sumter proved unsuccessful, the *Star* was to return immediately to Fortress Monroe and discharge her troops.

Rumors of the expedition to Anderson quickly spread through Washington. Secretary of the Interior Thompson, who had been sending assurances to Southern friends that no additional troops were to be sent to Sumter, angrily resigned when he learned of the *Star of the West.* "Government troops were sent on Saturday night from New York for Charleston," read one telegram that Pickens received on January 8.

"Mr. Thompson has been deceived by the Administration." Pickens had little time to prepare for the arrival of the *Star of the West*. He had set a trap, but could he spring it effectively?

"The one flag we longed to see"

On January 8, a boat from Charleston bearing employees of the Engineer Department made its daily landing at Fort Sumter. The workmen—local civilians whose loyalty to the Union had been cleared—had with them a Charleston newspaper which carried a story that a relief steamer was on its way to Sumter and would arrive that night. The paper was brought to Anderson, who refused to credit the unofficial account; besides, he reasoned, if Scott were sending him reinforcements, they would arrive aboard a man-o'-war, not a merchant vessel.

True, Anderson never received the letter giving him official notice of the expedition. But his officers seem to have been aware that help was coming; the rumors flew around the harbor thick as gulls. When the time came to test these rumors, Anderson was curiously hesitant. He had been heroically decisive in moving to Sumter, but once there his decisiveness seemed to give way. Perhaps, though only he and Elizabeth could have said, he now bitterly regretted having obeyed Scott's initial orders to relieve Colonel Gardiner. An attempt to bring reinforcements in to him now was almost certain to draw the fire of the Southern batteries; the United States flag would be fired upon. Hadn't he, after all, planned to take his family to Europe to sit out the war if it broke?

The *Star of the West* was nearing her destination. The trip had been easy; off the coast of North Carolina, Captain McGowan had stopped the ship for several hours while the men fished from the decks. At 1:30 on the morning of January 9 the ship arrived off the bar of Charleston Harbor, and McGowan surrendered the wheel to a pilot who knew the harbor. The engines were stopped, all lights were extinguished, and the ship drifted silently in the darkness. Before dawn, groping by frequent soundings, the pilot brought the ship to the entrance of the Morris Island channel. All harbor buoys and lights had been removed by Pickens' orders, and the ship had to be preceded by a pilot boat as she moved through the treacherous channel. When the first rays of daylight appeared in the eastern sky, the *Star of the West* was sighted by a small Southern patrol ship, which, after making a disregarded attempt to warn the *Star* away, headed for the bar, signaling wildly with rockets and colored lights. The batteries and shore installations had now been alerted.

As the sun rose, Captain Doubleday, standing his watch on Sumter's southeastern parapet and scanning the channel with his glasses, also sighted the *Star of the West* as she slowly approached Morris Island. He guessed that she was the rumored relief steamer and continued to follow her with his glasses as she neared the upper end of the island. The pilot boat sailed toward Sumter, raised and lowered the American flag at her masthead, and then headed back toward the *Star*. A few minutes after reveille, Sumter's garrison was animated by the news that a large steamer flying the Stars and Stripes was standing in the entrance of the harbor. The men rushed to the ramparts, leaving their breakfasts uneaten below. They were beginning to feel that they were a match for their adversaries and many of them hoped that the ship was indeed sent to bring reinforcements and not, as had also been rumored, to evacuate Sumter.

The *Star of the West* steamed on, headed toward the guns and black walls of Moultrie. Suddenly, as she passed near a group of houses close to the shore of Morris Island, her men spotted the red palmetto flag of a hidden battery among the sandhills. The next moment shells were flying across her bow, but falling wide. On Sumter the reaction to the puffs of blue smoke and the reports which reverberated across the otherwise silent harbor was instantaneous. Anderson gave orders to beat the long roll to summon the men to their battle stations and the men responded quickly, eager for action. They manned the only guns on the Morris Island side of the fort—three 24-pounders and one 8-inch seacoast howitzer—and replaced the already loaded grapeshot (intended to repel landing attempts) with solid shot.

At the first salvo from the hidden battery, a large United States flag had been quickly run up the forepeak of the *Star of the West* and then immediately lowered—the prearranged signal for Anderson to open fire on the opposing batteries. Anderson, never having received the crucial orders, could only watch this signal in puzzlement, and he restrained his men from opening fire. He attempted to acknowledge the enigmatic signal by having his own flag lowered, but the halyards had become twisted and could not be untangled. Shell fire was now heard from the direction of Moultrie, and Lieutenant Davis urged Anderson to return the fire. But he only received Anderson's consent for him to go down to the lower tier, take command of the two 42-pounders there, and await orders to fire.

The *Star of the West* continued on her course, a slow-moving target for the land batteries, whose wild and unskilled fire narrowly missed the pilothouse and walking beam. One spent shot lodged in the stern near her rudder, two feet above the waterline. "Why does not Major Anderson open fire on the battery and save us?" the New York *Evening Post* correspondent wrote in his notebook. "We look in vain for help. The American flag flies from Fort Sumter, and the American flag at our bow and stern is fired upon, yet there is not the slightest recognition of our presence from the fort to which we look for protection." The men stayed below decks with loaded muskets, waiting for the call to action. Some even began to wonder if the reason for Sumter's silence was that it had already been taken by the South Carolinians. But the American flag continued to fly above the fort, and Captain McGowan, despairing of further signals to Anderson, had his flag run up to the forepeak for good. The ship was now well within range of Moultrie's big guns, but, as Simons had bleakly predicted to Pickens, they had little effect on the *Star* as she

steamed against the powerful ebb tide. Not one shell
from Moultrie hit. And not one shot had so far been
fired from Sumter.

Aboard the *Star* Captain McGowan and Lieutenant
Woods were becoming increasingly alarmed by Anderson's silence and had a hurried consultation. They
both agreed it would be disastrous to try to run the
gauntlet of Southern batteries without protection from
Sumter. If the ship continued on her course through
the channel she would be less than 1,000 yards from
Fort Moultrie; and if she tried to enter the inner
harbor she would be exposed broadside to all of the
batteries lining the tip of Sullivan's Island. Mc-
Gowan and Woods felt that they had no choice but to
withdraw. McGowan lowered the flag, ordered full
steam, brought the ship around in the narrow part of
the channel, and started toward the open sea, once
again passing the hidden battery on Morris Island,
which again failed to do any damage.

Once in the ebb tide, the *Star of the West* was
swiftly carried out of range of the shore batteries.
Captain McGowan discovered minor damage on her
hull, due not so much to the barrage she had undergone but to the fact that as the tide had rapidly
fallen, her hull had scraped bottom three times. A
small Southern steamer followed the *Star of the West*
out of the channel, chasing her as a little fish would
a bigger one; she soon gave up the sport and returned
to Charleston.

As the *Star of the West* steamed away, the officers
at Sumter had to use all their authority to keep the
men from opening fire on Moultrie. Even the women
were swept away by the prevailing mood of anger and
frustration. The wife of Lieutenant Davis bared her

arm, took hold of a friction tube, and approached one of the guns. "You have a good deal of courage," Doubleday said to her as he gently drew her away from the gun.

An atmosphere of gloom settled over the garrison; morale had slipped. "Everything now looked more disheartening than before," Doubleday recalled. "The fort itself was a deep, dark, damp, gloomy-looking place, enclosed in high walls, where the sunlight rarely penetrated. If we ascended the parapet, we saw nothing but uncouth state flags, representing palmettos, pelicans, and other strange devices. Our glasses in vain swept the horizon; the one flag we longed to see had come at last, in a timid, apologetic way, and not as a representative of the war power of the Government."

Anderson now ordered the men back to their quarters, with the exception of two men to be stationed at each gun, and he called his perplexed and dejected officers together for a conference in a room originally intended as Sumter's laundry. Their flag had been fired upon and they had done nothing; what Anderson proposed now was to close the harbor and fire on any Southern ship which might from then on attempt to enter it. He solicited the view of his officers. Lieutenants Hall and Snyder registered agreement with Anderson's proposal. Meade said he thought they ought to wait; closing the harbor would be considered an act of war, and they had no right to make such a move. Lieutenant Davis also thought it best to wait and watch. But why not ask Pickens, he suggested, if the Governor officially avowed the gunfire from Moultrie and Morris islands. If Pickens did, only then should the harbor be closed and guarded with Sumter's guns.

Captain Doubleday was outspoken for immediate action, arguing that delay meant strength gained for the Secessionists. Surgeon Crawford stated frankly that he thought Anderson had let a magnificent opportunity slip by when he refused to return Moultrie's fire.

Major Anderson listened with interest to his officers. He seems to have preferred Lieutenant Davis' proposal, for he told them that he would write to Pickens and inform the Governor what he, Anderson, proposed to do if the Governor "avowed the act." Anderson sat down to draft a note to Pickens which he submitted to his officers for their approval:

> Two of your batteries fired this morning upon an unarmed vessel bearing the flag of my Government. As I have not been notified that war has been declared by South Carolina against the Government of the United States, I cannot but think that this hostile act was committed without your sanction and authority. Under that hope, and that alone, did I refrain from opening fire upon your batteries. I have, therefore, respectfully to ask whether the above-mentioned act, one I believe without a parallel in the history of our country or of any other civilized government, was committed in obedience to your instructions, and to notify you, if it not be disclaimed, that I must regard it as an act of war, and that I shall not, after a reasonable time for the return of my messenger, permit any vessel to pass within range of the guns of my fort. In order to save, as far as lies within my power, the shedding of blood, I beg that you will have due notice of this, my decision, given to all concerned. Hoping, however, that your answer may be such as will justify a further continuance of forbearance on my part.

The officers gave their approval, and the meeting ended. But Captain Foster was angry at what he considered Anderson's appeasing tone. He bounded up the stairs to the terreplein, two steps at a time, taking his temper out on his hat, which he crushed in his hands, and was overheard by another officer to say something about their flag's being trampled on. The men at their guns also overheard his angry soliloquy and had only to look at his disappointed expression to guess that the guns of Sumter would, for the time being, remain silent.

Lieutenant Hall, in full uniform and traveling under a white flag of truce, arrived in Charleston to deliver Anderson's note to Pickens. The usual excited crowd was there at the wharf to greet him, and it was only with difficulty that Hall reached Pickens' office in the Charleston Hotel. Told that the Governor was in council, Hall demanded an interview immediately.

In the short time since Hall's arrival, a wild rumor had aroused the city to a panic. The rumor assured everyone that Hall had come to tell Pickens Fort Sumter was about to bombard the city. Signs were hastily lettered informing the people of this threat. A band of frightened and angry Southerners rushed down to the harbor and milled around Hall's men, who waited there with the boat. The soldiers, who had been ordered not to talk with anyone, maintained silence and patiently and grimly withstood the threats of the near mob.

When Hall handed Anderson's letter over to Pickens, the Governor told him he would have to wait while he called his Cabinet together for discussion. The Cabinet discussion took about half an hour, Pick-

ens wrote out his answer, and Hall could now return
to Sumter. The always gallant Governor ordered the
Executive carriage brought around to take the lieutenant back to the boat, in the company of one of the
Governor's aides and an escort.

Major Anderson received Pickens' reply from Hall,
called his officers together, and read it aloud to them.

> The attempt to reinforce the troops in Fort
> Sumter, or to retake and resume possession of the
> forts within the water of this state, which you
> have abandoned, after spiking the guns placed
> there, and doing otherwise much damage, cannot
> be regarded by the authorities of this state as in-
> dicative of any other purpose than the coercion
> of the state by the armed force of the Govern-
> ment. To repel such an attempt is too plainly its
> duty. The *Star of the West* it is understood, this
> morning attempted to enter this harbor, with
> troops on board; and having been notified that she
> could not enter, was fired into. This act is per-
> fectly justified by me.

Pickens' answer not only avowed the attack on the
Star of the West but also made no attempt to apolo-
gize for it; the answer seemed openly hostile, putting
the next move up to Anderson. The major hesitated
still to take independent action and close the harbor,
but instead determined to sidestep the decision by sending a messenger to Washington with a report of the
situation and a request for orders—a mission he gave
to Lieutenant Talbot. For the second time that day
Anderson sent a letter to Pickens, to be delivered by
Talbot on his way through Charleston to the capital:

I have the honor to acknowledge the receipt of your communication of today, and to say that, under the circumstances, I have deemed it proper to refer the whole matter to my Government and that I intend following the course indicated in my note of this morning, until the arrival from Washington of the instructions I may receive. I have the honor, also, to express a hope that no obstructions will be placed in the way of, and that you will do me the favor to afford every facility to, the departure and return of the bearer, Lieutenant T. Talbot, United States Army, who has been directed to make the journey.

Talbot, in civilian clothes, left late in the afternoon, accompanied by Surgeon Crawford, in a boat carrying a conspicuous white flag. All was affable at the Charleston Hotel once the men were ushered into the Governor's office, where a Cabinet meeting was again in session. The encounter assumed an incongruously social tone. Talbot and Crawford were introduced to the Cabinet members, and the men stood around in friendly and cheerful conversation—a provocative scene in the circumstances. Talbot interpreted this friendly reception to mean that Pickens, too, had decided to delay action for the present. And for his part, Pickens was delighted that Talbot was going on this mission—every convenience would be placed at his disposal, including the Governor's carriage to take him to the railroad station.

Anderson had given the *Star of the West* no protection. The *S. S. Brooklyn,* her other hope, had also failed her. The *Brooklyn* finally showed up, just in time to escort the *Star* back to Fortress Monroe. January 9 had added no glory to Anderson; the North's cause appeared to have been held static by a man uncommitted to action and by a letter which was never delivered. In Washington a few days later, Judge Black meditated on the affair and found in it some reasons for hope. To him it suggested that it was entirely possible for a ship with a determined commander to run past the Southern batteries with only a fair chance of suffering serious damage. If the *Star of the West* episode proved anything, Black felt, it proved that the existing obstacles against the relief of Anderson were manageable: "I am convinced that a pirate, or a slaver, or a smuggler, who could be assured of making five hundred dollars by going into the harbor in the face of all the dangers which now threaten a vessel bearing the American flag, would laugh them to scorn!"

Judging the effect of the debacle on public opinion in the North, *The New York Times* commented: "The repulse of the *Star of the West* bearing reinforcements to Fort Sumter, and her precipitate retreat from the fire of the disunionists, have seriously stung the pride of the country. The silence and utter inactivity of the Government at Washington over this most direct and flagrant defiance of its authority create general disgust and indignation."

"Deficiencies in small stores"

Francis Pickens, though polite as a Carolina planter to Anderson's messenger, was profoundly troubled by the major's threat to close the harbor to all Southern vessels. The day after the *Star of the West* turned around and headed for the open sea, the Governor resumed his attempts to force the evacuation of Sumter. On January 10, in the Officer-of-the-Guard room at Sumter's sally port, two envoys from Pickens—Judge Magrath, Secretary of State for South Carolina, and General Jamison, State Secretary of War—presented Anderson and his officers with a firm demand to hand over the fort to the State authorities.

In front of the envoys, Anderson put a concise question to his officers: "Shall we accede to the demands of the Governor or shall we not?" The officers voted against yielding. "We will fire the magazine and be burned in common ruin before we shall surrender," declared Anderson to the envoys with typical nineteenth-century pyrotechnical bravado.

"Only God knows what the consequences will be," General Jamison pronounced in the same tone. Augmenting the drama, he continued: "There are twenty thousand men in South Carolina just spoiling to come down from the hills and tear the fort to pieces with their fingers. The waters of the harbor will be stained with their blood."

The grim prophecy failed to shake Anderson's decision; he knew perfectly well what his course must be. "I cannot do what belongs to the Government to do. The demand must be made to them. I appeal to you as a citizen, as a man, and as a fellow countryman, to do all that you can to prevent an appeal to arms. I do not say as a soldier, for my duty is plain in that respect." Anderson agreed to hold off making any decision about closing the harbor with Sumter's guns; he would wait until the Governor sent his own envoy to Washington to make one more effort at bringing around the Federal Government.

On the morning of January 11 this envoy, Isaac W. Hayne, Attorney General of the state of South Carolina, accompanied by Lieutenant Hall of Anderson's staff, boarded the train for Washington. Hayne had been fully briefed by Pickens; there were two courses open to him, both, it now seems, quite incredible in their presumption. He was to make a peremptory demand for Fort Sumter; if this demand were refused, he had the authority to offer to buy the fort from the Government. He carried with him a letter from Pickens, an ultimatum, explicitly giving the President of the United States the choice of promising not to reinforce Sumter or having his refusal considered as a declaration of war. Pickens could not have taken a stronger stand.

Hayne never let Buchanan see this letter, although he had an interview with him on January 14. Something made him hesitate, perhaps his own conviction that Pickens' immoderacy would be disastrous at this time. And then his personal doubts as to the sagacity of presenting the President with an ultimatum were bolstered by Senator Wigfall and his circle of Secessionist legislators in Washington. Making an accurate guess at the reasons for Hayne's presence in the capital, they persuaded Hayne to withhold the letter for the sake of the common good of all the Southern states; if Hayne acquiesced, Jefferson Davis' grand plan for a Southern Confederacy still had a chance. In their carefully reasoned letter to Pickens, Wigfall and his group wrote: "We think the state should suffer Major Anderson to obtain the necessary supply of food, fuel or water, and enjoy free communication, by post or special messenger with the President"—all this contingent on the President's promise not to send reinforcements.

Hayne agreed to withhold the letter—if they could obtain the President's promise. Shielding Pickens from the charge of overstepping his authority, Hayne misleadingly assured Wigfall that Anderson had free access to meat, vegetables, fuel and water.

Within the week, three of Wigfall's group requested an interview with Buchanan; they got to the second best, Secretary of War Holt. They showed him the letter they had written Hayne and asked for the Secretary's opinion on how they might obtain

Buchanan's assurance not to reinforce Sumter. "The President," Holt told them firmly, "has no authority to enter into such an agreement."

When Hayne tried to play his final card—an offer to purchase Sumter from the Government—he too met with a firm reply from Holt. "The proposal now presented to the President," Holt summed up sardonically, "is simply an offer on the part of South Carolina to buy Fort Sumter and its contents as a property of the United States, sustained by a declaration, in effect, that if she is not permitted to make the purchase, she will seize the fort by force of arms." In Holt's view, Buchanan could "no more sell or transfer Fort Sumter than he can sell the Capitol of the United States to Maryland."

Pickens' well-meaning ambassador had failed on both counts. He returned south having gained nothing but a new insight into the growing firmness and unfriendliness of the Federal Government. But nothing concrete had been done for Anderson either. The stalemate held.

"There is yet a single hope for freedom in the crisis," commented an editorial in the Chicago *Daily Tribune*. "If the South Carolinians would only make a determined assault upon Fort Sumter, level its walls to the sea, and slaughter its gallant commander and all his men, then perhaps the North would arise in vindication of the Constitution and the laws and teach the South that this country and government were not made for slaveholders. That is now almost our only hope."

At Sumter, the *Star of the West* debacle remained the chief topic of conversation among the officers. They awaited orders from Washington but they were certain that regardless of the outcome of the missions of Talbot, Hall and Hayne, Pickens would continue his active operations against the fort. The soldier Anderson, with years of experience behind him, worked tirelessly to prepare the fort for any eventuality. With his engineer officer, Captain James Foster, he set about the work of defense.

They tackled Sumter's heavy armament. A few large guns were already mounted on the parapet and lower tier, but many were still lying on the parade like castoff shoes. While some of the men were put to work preparing to hoist the heavy barrels to their stations, others made gun platforms and refitted the carriages necessary to support the cannon. "Hand grenades" were made by filling 8-inch shells with powder and then inserting friction tubes attached to long lanyards. As each grenade was finished, a man carried it to the parapet and stored it along the base of the wall. In the event of attack the grenade could simply be dropped over the parapet by one man who would explode it by pulling on the lanyard. Powder bags were needed for the big columbiads; another group of men was busy preparing them. As a substitute for silk powder bags—a scarce item—the men used all the flannel shirts they could get from the quartermaster; Anderson contributed his socks, then set the men to work on making the bags with the fort's six needles.

In the main gate a group of men completed a solid wall of masonry, three feet thick, with a narrow space left for a passageway and as an embrasure for the 8-inch howitzer placed there to sweep the wharf with direct fire. Two heavy guns were mounted to the right and left of the sally port, their lanyards trailing inside the walls so they could be fired in safety.

Sumter had no flanking defense, but Captain Doubleday constructed one ingeniously from his imagination and the tools at hand; great "dry-goods" boxes were hung over the parapets three or four feet, their huge supporting beams extending inward to the terreplein and securely anchored.

To meet the possibility of a rush against the walls, Anderson assigned two sharpshooters to each gallery. Against a determined close assault he would use small hand grenades, similar in construction and operation to the large ones. If the fort were attacked by way of the wharf, the invaders would have a perilous trip to the walls; Anderson had the wharf mined. He tried to meet every possible avenue and method of attack by constructing defenses to combat them.

The weakest point of defense of the entire fort was the gorge and esplanade, which could be especially inviting to an enterprising storming party. The esplanade was a broad walk of dressed granite running the entire length of the gorge wall. Anderson set a series of medieval booby-traps on this promenade. They looked like harmless piles of stones resting against the scarp wall, but underneath each was concealed a magazine of gunpowder with a trigger mechanism, which, when manipulated from inside the walls, would explode lethally. Anderson also had two 8-inch howitzers mounted so as to be able to sweep, in a crossfire arrangement, the entire esplanade.

To reinforce the gorge wall, which was studded with windows and ventilators, Anderson had his men place solid iron jambs in the second-tier windows. The doors on the lower tier were closed with heavy wooden shutters protected in front by rocks wedged in with molten lead and backed by a brick wall nine inches thick. Protection for the hospital and ordnance room was also increased.

But there was still one spot, a chink in the fort's armor, where a thousand men could have stood and been perfectly safe from fire coming from any direction. It was there, between the high scarp wall and the tidewater, that Anderson had large granite stones rolled to cover the ripraps. The job was back-breaking; when it was finished an additional eight or nine feet of elevation put a landing place out of reach of the attackers.

Captain Seymour, borrowing from the idea of the booby-traps placed on the esplanade, constructed a weapon he called the "Flying Fougasse"—an ordinary wooden barrel inside of which nestled a canister of powder and small stones. If the barrel were rolled over the parapet and a lanyard pulled, the whole thing would blow up in the enemy's face.

When the first Flying Fougasse was finished, the entire garrison assembled on the parapet to watch it being tested. Across the water at Moultrie, South Carolina officers, having got wind of the test, apprehensively focused their glasses on Sumter. At a signal, the barrel was rolled over the edge. A tremendous explosion followed; stones were hurled against the walls of the fort and some distance out into the channel. The effect was a psychological boon for Anderson. The Charleston papers declared that the Flying Fougasse—in reality just a barrel of powder and stones—was "an infernal machine, simply terrific." Anderson was gratified by the mechanical and psychological effect of the tests; he took advantage of them both and placed empty barrels along the parapet, like scarecrows in a field.

Most of the guns were in position but their accuracy could not be depended on because, although the men had plenty of rammers, sponge staffs, hand spikes and tongs for carrying shells, only a few breech sights, two quadrants and one gunner's level could be found. Fortunately for Anderson, some of his officers were experienced artillery men with a flair for improvisation. Among other pieces, they devised a "pointing rod" which would enable gunners to make quick and accurate changes in the elevation of the guns. Doubleday, Chester and Anderson worked in the moonlight to make sure that the men would be able to fire in the dark. They carefully aimed every gun in the fort at all the targets in its field of fire and marked the position on the traverse circle, the track which bore the wheels of the carriage; they then fastened an indicator to the traverse fork which seemingly made alignment as easy as setting a watch.

Anderson's number-one problem, defense, was slowly being resolved by ingenuity and back-breaking work. Problem number two, lack of fighting manpower, was not soluble; he simply had to make do with what he had—seventy men. After some study, Anderson and his officers estimated that only eight men could be stationed at each flank of the fort, leaving about twenty men as reserves. Sumter had been planned for a garrison of 650 men. And yet, Sumter was appraised by the Charleston *Mercury* to be "The Bastion of the Federal Union. The Fate of the Southern Confederacy hangs by the halyards of Fort Sumter."

The weather grew more severe. The rain was chill and fog closed in around the walls. Anderson decided to move the entire garrison into the recently completed and relatively weathertight officers' quarters. But clothing and fuel shortages were beginning to tell. For firewood the men had to tear down the temporary buildings on the parade ground. By the end of January, with winter's end not yet in sight, there were only two outbuildings and twelve wooden gun carriages left for fuel.

The men had subsisted for weeks without sufficient fresh meat and vegetables. Since late in December, when Pickens had prevented Lieutenant Snyder from bringing provisions back to Sumter, the army's food contractor in Charleston had steadily refused to do any business with Anderson. The merchant feared boycott and reprisals from the citizens of Charleston if he were to yield to Anderson's appeals. It was only through the stratagems of Anderson's Charleston friend, Robert Gourdin, that occasional supplies were smuggled in—but not in sufficient quantities to solve the problem. While Talbot was absent in Washington, Anderson asked Surgeon Crawford to inspect and make an inventory of the stores and provisions on hand. "Instead of six months' supply," Crawford reported, "there is scarcely four"; now "deficiencies in small stores" were felt. Crawford told Anderson that he would have to place the men on half-rations of coffee and sugar and deprive the officers of these items altogether for the time being. The commissary was completely out of soap and candles. Lights were improvised by setting a wick in an eating bowl filled with lighthouse oil.

In addition to the problems of food and supplies, Anderson had to cope with fifth-column activities Pickens' agents were carrying on among the civilian workers who came to the fort. Some of the workers had already disaffected, leaving forty-three who seemed to be loyal to Anderson. In Charleston reports were circulated that Anderson was holding workmen at the fort against their will. This rumor grew to such proportions that a civil court in Charleston called Lieutenant Davis and four enlisted men to testify in a case in which the fort had been charged with coercing workmen. Why Anderson allowed his men to appear at all in the court is a mystery. At any rate, the charges were not proved and the case was dismissed. A rumor of mutiny in the garrison was stilled by a letter from Doubleday published in Northern papers.

Another story spread by Pickens' agents was especially vicious and was designed to alienate Anderson's supporters in the North. One of Anderson's men, the fiction ran, was in league with a relative in Charleston to betray the fort. Anderson, discovering the treachery, was supposed to have condemned the traitor to death. A priest was summoned, ostensibly to attend to a sick woman, but his real business was to administer the sacraments to the culprit and prepare him for execution. Anderson, the story concluded, had the traitor ignominiously hanged at the fort. The tale was widely believed and was carried, in some detail, in a New York newspaper.

On January 19, Lieutenant Talbot returned from Washington with a dispatch for Anderson. Secretary of War Holt's letter contained the first definite instructions Anderson had so far received and an implicit apology for the Government's failure to inform Anderson of the imminent relief expedition:

You rightly designated the firing into the *Star of the West* as an "act of war" and one which was actually committed without the slightest provocation. Had their act been perpetrated by a foreign nation, it would have been your imperative duty to have resisted it with the whole force of your batteries. As, however, it was the work of the Government of South Carolina and was prompted by the passions of a highly inflamed population of citizens of the United States, your forbearance to return the fire is fully approved by the President. Unfortunately, the Government had not been able to make known to you that the *Star of the West* had sailed from New York for your relief and hence, when she made her appearance in the harbor of Charleston, you did not feel the force of your obligation to protect her approach as you would naturally have done had this information reached you.

Your late dispatches, as well as the very intelligent statement of Lieutenant Talbot, have relieved the Government of the apprehensions recently entertained for your safety. In consequence, it is not its purpose at present to reinforce you. The attempt to do so would, no doubt, be attended by a collision of arms and the effusion of blood—a national calamity which the President is most anxious, if possible, to avoid. You will, therefore, report frequently your condition, and the character and activity of the preparations, if any, which may be being made for an attack upon the fort, or for obstructing the Government in any endeavors it may make to strengthen your command.

Holt concluded the letter by asking Anderson to use special messenger instead of mail when he saw fit; if Anderson were to ask for supplies and reinforcements from the War Department, Holt wrote, "a prompt and vigorous effort will be made to forward them."

Although it contained no promise of immediate relief, the letter from Holt did not preclude it. It was also an endorsement of the major's stand.

That same morning, the 19th, the Quartermaster General of the state of South Carolina, under orders from Judge Magrath, started assembling a forty-eight-hour supply of meat and vegetables for the men at Sumter. The boat carrying the precious cargo drew up at Sumter's wharf at noon the next day. The men rushed to the boat and began unloading her without waiting for orders; they had not seen such an abundance of food since their move from Moultrie. Within a few minutes Anderson had heard of the food's arrival and ordered his soldiers to stop unloading and to return to the boat what they had already carried inside the fort. He was angered by the report, spread by Hayne and apparently accepted in Washington, that his garrison was receiving daily supplies of food; he was unwilling to lend substance to this untruth and to accept an act of what he thought charity. The men obeyed his orders. "So many acts of harshness and incivility" had occurred since his move to Sumter, he wrote to Washington, that he felt unable to accept any favors from South Carolina. "The Governor was influenced solely by considerations of courtesy," a spokesman for Pickens said, in explanation, when the boat returned to Charleston.

Anderson's men continued hungry for the food they needed, but Anderson now had to turn to another problem that demanded his attention—the women and children at the fort, who not only put a strain on the food supply but hindered work and would be in danger in case of an attack. In response to Anderson's request that the women and children be allowed to leave on a New York steamer that he would arrange for, Pickens answered that he would provide every facility in his power. An agent for the Northern steamship company shortly afterward visited the fort and told Anderson to have the forty-two women and children ready to leave on February 1, when a steamer would appear in Charleston Harbor to take them to New York.

Pickens' attempts at gallantry in sending fresh food and agreeing to the removal of the women and children coincided rather than contrasted with his own continuing military preparations; still holding an essentially romantic, chivalric view of warfare, he could be both relentless and courtly and see no contradiction. Although Hayne's unsuccessful mission to Washington had forced him to realize that South Carolina could not act as an independent nation and must bide her time until the formation of a Confederacy, he went ahead with the construction of his war machine, and even brought it more into the open. One day, perhaps, when the Southern Confederacy was established, his initiative and genius as a military planner would be recognized, he convinced himself.

Pickens and his military engineers decided that a surprise attack on Fort Sumter would cost the lives of too many of their own men. So they agreed on a plan to soften Sumter by pounding away at her with heavy batteries until she was too weak to resist landing parties. To this end Pickens secured appropriations for the construction of a floating battery, large enough to carry six heavy guns, and for the strengthening of all the forts and batteries in the harbor. Day and night boats carrying guns, munitions and men sailed back and forth across the harbor in plain sight of Sumter's garrison. Negro slaves did much of the heavy work on the fortifications, building up the walls of Moultrie, erecting heavy shields for the guns there, mounting additional guns there and at Cummings Point, Fort Johnson and Morris Island.

On January 29, for no apparent reason, the batteries on Morris Island opened fire. Immediately, in response, the other forts in the harbor sent up rocket signals which were in turn answered by signals from the harbor steamers. Before long the men at Sumter saw guard boats entering the harbor escorted by two tugs. Shortly after midnight, guns again sounded, this time from Moultrie. Anderson could only suppose that a steamer or possibly a warship was trying to enter the harbor. But nothing was ever seen. The little incident, a false alarm, showed Anderson how rapidly Pickens' batteries and ships would communicate an alarm to one another and how effectively they might work together against any future relief expedition.

"The President declared to a member of Congress that he had no doubt that Fort Sumter would be attacked in less than a week," *The New York Times* reported on January 31. "The congressman inquired why he did not reinforce Major Anderson. The President replied that there were not enough vessels in the American Navy to reach Fort Sumter. Letters are received from Fort Sumter as late as the 26th, stating that all the officers and men are well. While they would like some fresh meat for a change, they are united in feeling against succumbing to the terms of the Charleston authorities."

CHAPTER
TEN

"I am in the hands of God"

On the morning of February 1, the evacuation of Sumter's women and children began. As arranged by Anderson, a steamer was waiting for them in Charleston, and as the families of the enlisted men crowded about the wharf, watching their baggage being carried aboard the barge, the conversations of farewell neared their end. One soldier who wrote an account of this morning was affected enough by the occasion to remember it in the language of the melodrama of the time. The parting was, he wrote, "a distressing contingency, attended by smothered tears and sighs." "We have been married seven years," he reported one woman as saying to her husband, "and I never had a reason to find fault with you. Now, whatever may happen, I know I shall never have cause to blush for you." "I don't want you to think of us," another said. "The children and myself will get along, and you'll have enough to think about here." Despite the sentimental conventions of the dialogue, the scene is clear: neither husbands nor wives had any certainty that they would see each other again.

When the last passenger was aboard, lines were cast off and the barge was towed to Charleston, where the passengers transferred to the steamer. After an unaccountable delay of two days, at noon on February 3 the steamer cleared for New York and passed under the guns of Sumter. Anderson gave his consent for a salute to be fired. The men lingered on the parapet until the steamer had vanished over the horizon.

With the families of his soldiers safely on their way home, Anderson put his men back to work on the defenses of the fort. The February weather was clear, and from the walls of Sumter could be seen the continuing work on the other forts in the harbor. The civilian workmen brought the garrison daily reports of Charleston—regiments turned out to parade and drill, the citizens of the city promenading ostentatiously in the mild sunlight. As the men heard these reports day after day, their anger, apprehensiveness and defiance mounted, and they finally prevailed on Anderson to let them fire a token shot in the direction of the city. Anderson ordered one of the big cannon to be loaded and fired. "The report startled the bold recruits ashore," wrote one of Anderson's men, "and when the shell struck it sent a spray to the housetops and lashed the water into foam for several hundred yards."

But such a demonstration as this could not divert either Anderson or the men from the realization that the power against Sumter seemed to be building up to

a terrifying aggregation. The Cummings Point battery, which mounted both mortars and heavy guns
bearing on the gorge of Sumter, was now practically
bombproof; the guns were protected under a shield of
iron backed by wooden beams—a shield impervious to
Anderson's armament. Pickens' floating battery was
nearly complete, and Anderson was concerned enough
to write to Washington for directions in the event the
battery should approach the fort. He was ordered to
act with forbearance, the likelihood being, as Holt
wrote him, "that there will be no immediate attack
on Fort Sumter."

There were now 89 guns bearing on Fort Sumter.
In addition to the powerful batteries at Moultrie, Sullivan's Island, Morris Island and Fort Johnson, Anderson learned of something even more formidable: a
Blakely rifled cannon, recently arrived from England
and mounted at Cummings Point. Capable of throwing a twelve-pound shell with great force and accuracy, it could quickly breech and reduce the walls of
Sumter. The new gun was the gift of a Charlestonian
who had it sent over from England, and it bore an
inscription on its polished barrel: "Presented to the
State of South Carolina by a citizen resident abroad,
in commemoration of December 20th, 1860."

Although powerless to counter these armaments and
the swelling ranks of armed Southern recruits, Anderson doggedly kept on with the daily work of cement-
ing broken casemates, moving and testing the guns, in-
ventorying his dwindling supplies, and making reports
to Washington. But he still found time for a few
diversions. On February 8 he sat for the Charleston photographer, George Cook, who had formerly
worked for the renowned Washington society photog-

rapher, Mathew B. Brady. At the request of his
friend, Surgeon Crawford, Anderson posed for a
half-length picture, in his uniform but without his
hat.

At noon on February 22, Washington's birthday—
a day on which Buchanan, fearful of demonstrations,
very nearly canceled the traditional parade in the capital—Anderson ordered the barbette guns manned, and,
despite the shortage of ammunition and powder bags,
Sumter fired the national salute, one shot for each of
the original thirteen states. But the gesture had its de-
structive effects. The fort's supply of rice, which had
been soaked in a rainstorm some days before, was lying spread out to dry on the upper floor of the unused
officers' quarters. The holiday salute shattered a win-
dow, which showered the drying rice with splinters of
glass. Anderson immediately ordered the rice sifted,
but in the process some of the precious grain was lost.

Provisions dwindled, despite occasional gifts by
mail from Northern supporters of delicacies and such
staples as solidified milk, and Anderson's dispatches
to Washington made insistent reference to Sumter's
impoverished larder. The meager diet and the lack of
sleep were beginning to undermine his health and
spirits. He became depressed and morose. "I am in
the hands of God," he said to Crawford. He was
somewhat encouraged by the flow of letters from the
North, some proffering money for the support of the
soldiers' families. But he could not forget that what
he needed was men, cartridge bags, ships and food.

The threats they read every day in the Charleston
journals, the ever-present thought that their Government had deserted them—all worked to dull the garrison's morale. The weakness of the fort in the face of

a battering attack and the imminent, seemingly inevitable battle were always in Anderson's mind and
were subjects discussed constantly among his men.
They talked and speculated and asked one another the
same questions over and over again, but no one had the
answers.

It was during this discouraging period that Anderson received an order from Secretary of War Holt,
dated February 23, which increased his feelings of fu-
tility and powerlessness and was indeed to compel him
to inaction during a coming crisis. "You will continue," the orders read, "as heretofore, to act strictly
on the defensive, and to avoid, by all means compati-
ble with the safety of your command, a collision with
the hostile forces by which you are surrounded. The
policy thus indicated must still govern your conduct."
Anderson took these instructions literally though with
some reluctance; they left him, he felt, little discretion
to act in case of emergency. "The policy thus indicated" was another part of the legacy of a President
who wished most deeply to avoid collision.

On February 28 Anderson called his ten officers together for a conference, the most important one they
had had since the firing on the *Star of the West*.
When they had all assembled in his quarters, Anderson
announced that he wanted from each man a written
estimate of the force he thought necessary to break the
deadlock in Charleston Harbor by retaking Moultrie,
Pinckney and other installations and consolidating the
Union positions. Anderson instructed them not to consult with one another but to go back to their posts or
quarters, write their reports, and turn them in as
quickly as possible.

An hour or so later Anderson had all the reports

and began to examine them. They varied as to the number of men and ships needed, but all agreed that naval support was vitally necessary. Captain Foster estimated that 10,000 regulars or 30,000 recruits could storm and hold the key installations in the harbor. Lieutenant Snyder thought that 4,000 regulars and four naval vessels could accomplish this, and Crawford and Lieutenant Meade also gave roughly this estimate. The rest of the reports specified between 3,000 and 4,000 regulars and not less than six naval vessels. Captain Doubleday's estimate was the lowest: 1,000 regulars with naval support.

Anderson thanked his officers and sat down to evaluate their reports. When he had finished he wrote his dispatch to the War Department: "I confess that I would not be willing to risk my reputation on an attempt to throw reinforcements into this harbor within the time for our relief rendered necessary by the limited supply of our provisions, with a force of not less than 20,000 good and well-disciplined men." These men were to be brought in on transports with a full escort of armed naval vessels. Anderson had carefully considered the estimates given by his officers, but in citing the high figure of 20,000, as in every other choice to be made at Sumter, he made the final decision. The disparity between this startlingly high estimate and his earlier statement that the Government could send troops at its leisure was to trouble the incoming Lincoln administration and to haunt Anderson's later years.

On the morning of March 1, Governor Francis Pickens rose early, breakfasted, and entered the Executive Office he had established in the Charleston Hotel. He was not in the best of humor. In the weeks since he had sent Hayne on his futile mission to Washington, he had been under fire from many quarters. The Wigfall group in Washington had rebuked him for his impetuousness; the Charleston papers, still optimistic that South Carolina would seize the initiative by herself, continued to criticize him for not ordering a bold and decisive move against Sumter. Even this "most daring revolutionist of them all," as John G. Nicolay later called Pickens, had begun to realize the advantage to be gained by an over-all, common government of all the seceding states. He had deliberately slackened his efforts toward making South Carolina independent and counted on the imminent Confederacy to assume the responsibility he had been carrying by himself.

On February 4, the provisional government of the Confederacy had been established at Montgomery, Alabama, and on February 8 Jefferson Davis of Mississippi was elected its President; Alexander H. Stephens of Georgia became Vice President. The next day Pickens received orders from the Confederate Secretary of State, Robert Toombs, not to attack Fort Sumter "without the sanction and jurisdiction of our joint Government." Although Pickens accepted the higher authority of the Confederacy, there were still flashes of defiant independence. "I hope to be ready by Friday," he telegraphed Toombs on February 12, "and I think I am ready to take Fort Sumter or silence it"; but nothing came of this.

By February 22, the Confederate Congress had approved a resolution to take charge of all military operations within the seceding states, and Captain W. H. C. Whiting reported to Pickens that he had been ordered to inspect the harbor and the installations and discover as much as he could about Pickens' defenses. The military survey was as humiliating and as pessimistic as General Simons' had been in its findings. Whiting disapproved of almost everything Pickens' engineers had done so far and reported "an alarming description of affairs." The troops were green, poorly equipped, indifferently organized, and no match for veteran soldiers. The men at the batteries, formidable though their guns were, had had little experience in handling them and could, Whiting believed, be easily outgunned by Anderson's veteran artillerists. Pickens and his military enthusiasts had devoted themselves entirely to the reduction of Fort Sumter and had given little thought to a possible Federal attack on the harbor or a determined relief expedition.

Pickens and his officials were stunned and embarrassed by the report and the citizens of Charleston found an outlet for their disappointment in demanding the removal of Whiting. "Enthusiasm and unanimity of purpose," the *Mercury* wistfully declared, "largely compensate for many deficiencies in experience and materials."

Pickens had not only been thwarted and criticized but he had begun to feel that his own hoped-for role as a military leader was in doubt. His request for specific orders from Montgomery as to a proposed attack on Sumter had gone unanswered, and the Governor fumed at the delay. Now, on the morning of March 1, his role was clarified. An orderly brought him a telegram from the Confederate Secretary of War, Leroy Pope Walker:

"Your letter to the President received. This Government assumes control of military operations at Charleston, and will make demand of the fort when fully advised. An officer goes tonight to take charge."

That evening the unnamed officer, Brigadier General Pierre Gustave Toutant Beauregard, recently of the United States Army, took the night train from Montgomery for Charleston.

On March 4, Abraham Lincoln was inaugurated sixteenth President of the United States. Washington hotels and rooming houses were so overcrowded that hundreds had to find places to sleep on the porches of private houses, on sidewalks and in the hallways of public buildings. More than 25,000 strangers roamed the city's streets and milled around Willard's Hotel, the most famous hotel in Washington. There had been rumors of violence against the person of the President-elect, and General Scott had placed squads of riflemen on the rooftops and in windows along Pennsylvania Avenue with orders to fire on anyone who might menace the Presidential carriage. By noon, his affairs in order, President Buchanan drove to Willard's in an open barouche, accompanied by Senator Baker and Senator Pearce, to call for Lincoln.

When they arrived at the hotel, Buchanan stepped out of the carriage and disappeared inside, returning a few moments later arm in arm with Lincoln. The two men walked the path cleared for them by the cordon of policemen to the carriage and the procession made its way down Pennsylvania Avenue. At the Capitol, in the Senate chamber, they witnessed the swearing in of Hannibal Hamlin of Maine as Vice President. Then a new procession was formed to escort Lincoln to the platform outside the East Portico for the ceremony. A crowd of more than ten thousand, who had been waiting all morning, cheered. Upstairs, in the windows of the Capitol, on each side of the inaugural platform, Scott's riflemen surveyed the audience. On a high eminence in back of the platform, the actor John Wilkes Booth leaned over the rail and watched the proceedings, caught in eternal sullenness by the camera of Mathew Brady.

Lincoln, in a new black suit, black boots and black top hat and carrying an ebony and gold-headed cane, took his seat. Edward Dickinson Baker, the senator from Oregon, stepped forward. "Fellow citizens, I introduce to you Abraham Lincoln, the President-elect of the United States." There was some light applause as Lincoln rose to deliver his inaugural address. "In your hands, my dissatisfied fellow countrymen, and not in mine, is the momentous issue of civil war," he concluded. "The Government will not assail you. You can have no conflict without being yourselves the aggressors. *You* have no oath registered in Heaven to destroy the Government, while *I* shall have the most solemn one to 'preserve, protect, and defend it.'"

"To twenty millions of people," wrote the New York *Tribune* of Lincoln's inaugural address, "it will carry tidings, good or not, as the case may be, that the Federal Government of the United States is still in existence, with a Man at the head of it."

Chief Justice Roger Brooke Taney, famed for his Dred Scott decision, with the face of a walking corpse, opened a Bible and held it out with a shaking hand. Lincoln laid his left hand on the Bible, raised his right hand and repeated the oath after the Chief Justice. A battery of cannon thundered a salute to the sixteenth President of the United States. When the ceremony was over, Buchanan spoke his last words to the new President as they rode together to the White House from the Inauguration: "If you are as happy, my dear sir, on entering this house as I am in leaving it and returning home, you are the happiest man in this country."

CHAPTER
ELEVEN

"We salute the North with our Beau-regard"

What the people of Charleston needed now was a leader who would conform to their romantic notions and represent, as Pickens could not, the kind of hero born to challenge the major guarding his island fortress. This leader, dominating and aristocratic, appeared on the afternoon of March 3 in the person of Brigadier General Pierre Gustave Toutant Beauregard, late of the Engineers of the United States Army.

Beauregard was from Louisiana, a Creole; his olive complexion, broad brow and high cheekbones set him apart from other men. A continual expression of disdain controlled his features. Jet-black hair, a meticulous mustache and a perfect tiny goatee topped this walking Napoleonic marshal. One year later, Beauregard's hair had turned white; some said worry was responsible, others blamed the Federal blockade which had prevented ships carrying, among other things, hair dyes from reaching the South.

Beauregard's eyes were impressive to some, to others they seemed like the sad eyes of a bloodhound. But few failed to recognize in him the epitome of the Southern gentleman turned hero for a cause; few failed to recognize that his imperious nature, which was fed by the adulation of his superiors as well as that of the common citizen, was gifted with resourcefulness, industry and first-class military engineering.

Almost from the minute Beauregard stepped off the train from Montgomery, he was cast in a hero's role. His Creole ancestry stimulated the invention of tales of his supposed immorality (one version had it that he always traveled with a harem and a wagonload of champagne). He remained a figure of attractive mystery and worldliness. The women of Charleston worshiped him and kept him oversupplied with fresh flowers, gifts of flags, scarves, even escritoires; his suite at the Charleston Hotel looked more like a salon or florist's shop than a military headquarters. He worked in the midst of a crowd of officers, messengers, and orderlies; politicians, senators, and planters served as voluntary aides. He was popular beyond description, and he was celebrated in doggerel rhymes:

With cannon and musket, with shell and petard,
We salute the North with our Beau-regard.

The grave brigadier general had been a student in Major Anderson's class in artillery at West Point. He was graduated second in a class of forty-five and even stayed on at the Point for a while as an Assistant Instructor of Artillery. He served on General Winfield Scott's staff in the Mexican War, during which he was twice wounded and twice brevetted, first captain, then major, for meritorious conduct at the battles of Contreras and Churubusco. Like Anderson, then, he served with great distinction in the Mexican War, but, unlike his adversary, he was still full of confidence, boldly certain of his own ability, and not the least torn by divided loyalties.

With Beauregard's arrival in Charleston, two noticeable changes took place: the harbor fortifications began to look more terrifying to Anderson and the Confederate soldiers shaved off their beards, adopting instead mustache and goatee, like their idol.

The new general's first official act was a tour of inspection of the entire complex of fortifications. Accompanied by Whiting, now his engineer officer, Beauregard at once recognized that Sumter was, in his words, "a perfect Gibraltar." He condemned the works on Morris Island as untenable and criticized the crowding of guns and merlons at Cummings Point. He also discovered that the works there had been constructed for the sole purpose of reducing Sumter without regard to the fact that the channel was thus left unguarded.

Established in luxury in his headquarters, near Pickens' suite, Beauregard set to work. He had two main plans: to prevent any naval expedition from relieving Anderson, and to reduce Sumter by bombardment. His immediate tactics were to form a ring of mortar batteries around Sumter from which his men could lob shells into the stronghold as easily as tossing pennies into a silk hat. Beauregard was certain that Washington would never give up the fort without a battle. There, three and a third miles away, sat Anderson, like Cerberus at the gates of Hell, guarding the very sym-

bol of Confederate ambitions. Beauregard was determined to throw all he could muster at his former instructor. He wired to the Confederate Government at
Montgomery for more guns and started putting local
engineers to work experimenting with various machines
of war.

Governor Pickens, like his constituents, was delighted with this captivating General. Pickens persuaded the Confederate Government to widen the
scope of Beauregard's command to include the entire coastal area of South Carolina. The aristocratic
Beauregard was having a fine time organizing the
preparations for assault and mingling with the city's
first families. "I am very well pleased with this place
and its people who are so much like ours in Louisiana
that I see little difference," he wrote in a letter home.

Between them Pickens and Beauregard engineered
the sealing off of Anderson. When Sumter fell, they
assured each other, everything now standing in the
way of the Confederacy would collapse with it.

Anderson and his men were not unaware that
the character of the fortifications bristling around them
was changing. Captain Foster stood at the parapet for
hours with a pad and pencil, making surprisingly
accurate sketches of the enemy's works. Every messenger that came to the fort was questioned; Charleston newspapers, which carried precise descriptions of
the installations, were eagerly read for information.

Captain Foster was especially concerned about
Cummings Point, where he observed that several
steamerloads of men had landed. The men there could
be seen huddled about bivouac fires, without shelters,
trying to keep warm in weather that was mean with
cold March winds from the north.

Foster reported to Washington that he had learned
that portable hot-shot furnaces had been furnished to
several and probably all of the Southern batteries.
"The mortar battery on James Island, south of Fort
Johnson, is armed, but the number of mortars is not as-
certained," he wrote. He completed the report with a
detailed description of the enemy's strength in guns
at Sullivan's Island, Fort Moultrie and Morris Island.
It was considerable.

On March 9, Anderson, visibly anxious at his
growing isolation, wrote this report to Washington:

> I have the honor to report that we can see the
> South Carolinians engaged this morning strength-
> ening and extending considerably what we sup-
> posed to have been intended for a mortar battery
> at Fort Johnson. Small parties are also working at
> Nos. 9 and 10, and a very heavy force at the bend
> of the island, this side of No. 1. Whether they are
> constructing another battery there or strengthen-
> ing one that is already there I cannot tell.

Beauregard now assumed command of all regular and volunteer troops on duty in Charleston Harbor—an aggregate of 8,835 men. In Montgomery, the
men of the Confederacy were growing apprehensive
lest reinforcements should reach Sumter before the
South was ready. On March 9 they told Beauregard
to carry out his "contemplated works with all possible
expedition."

A prophetic incident occurred at Sumter six days
later. It was late in the evening. The sharp eyes of
the men on guard suddenly espied a canoe making
for the fort. When the boat reached the wharf, a

young Negro jumped out, walked through the sally
port, and, in the course of questioning by an officer, revealed that he was a slave, run away from his master
in Charleston. He had come to Sumter, he said, in a
stolen canoe in order to join the United States Army.
The account amused the officers, but they made light
of it and sent the man back that night. This slave
foreshadowed the thousands of "contrabands," as
they were known, who later joined the Union forces
as muleteers and teamsters, orderlies and cooks. There
is no record of Anderson's reaction to the incident.

On March 5 Lincoln had received Anderson's
request for a relief expedition and his estimate that
20,000 men and a fleet of war vessels would be
needed. How could he, Lincoln wondered, reconcile
this with an earlier dispatch from the major to the
effect that Sumter had sufficient provisions and men
and that "we can hold our own as long as it is
necessary to do so?" What was the true condition of
the fort's supplies? Could Anderson be counted on?

Lincoln went to Secretary Holt and privately asked
if Holt had any reason to doubt Anderson's loyalty. Holt said no. Rumors and doubts still multiplied;
the New York *Herald* reported, "It would be useless
to deny the fact that it is whispered in executive cir-
cles that Major Anderson is suspected of complicity
with the Secessionists of South Carolina."

New at his job, unsure of his associates, thrown
into a situation requiring tact and a great deal of precise information, Lincoln was discovering that his
pre-inauguration pledge to "hold, occupy, and possess
the property and places belonging to the Government"
was not going to be accomplished easily or straight-
forwardly. He was also beginning to have an ink-

ling that the gallant major in his isolated stronghold might very well give him conflicting reports, according to how optimistic he felt when he sat down to write them.

The new President called a Cabinet meeting for March 15 to discuss Anderson's crisis with his military advisers, hoping to find a way to break through the curtain of mystery that hung at the harbor's entrance. The Cabinet members were introduced to Captain Gustavus Vasa Fox, a career naval officer who had proposed a plan early in January to General Scott. Fox's plan, which Scott approved but Buchanan failed to authorize, was simple: troops and provisions were to be put aboard a large steamer along with a crew and three hundred extra sailors and armed launches, enough men and equipment to land the troops safely at Sumter in a single night. The steamer was to ship in a convoy with a warship escort and two powerful seagoing tugs, protected with cotton bales; the tugs were to transport the troops and provisions from the bar at Charleston Harbor to the fort.

Lincoln liked Fox's plan, he informed his Cabinet, and in their presence wrote out the following question, to which he asked them to reply, also in writing: "Assuming it to be possible to provision Fort Sumter, is it wise under all the circumstances of the case to attempt to do so?" Five members of the Cabinet answered negatively, only two advocating a try. The new Secretary of State and the most influential man both in the Cabinet and the Republican party, William H. Seward, reflected the majority opinion, and, incidentally that of his chief; his reply argued that any possible relief would be only temporary, that a failure could be disastrous and mean the eventual loss of the fort. Lincoln terminated the meeting without having taken a decisive step in any direction.

Still in the role of cautious investigator, Lincoln made up his mind to send two men to Sumter—one officially, one as a private envoy—to size up the situation and report to him. The first was Gustavus Fox, chosen by General Scott, on Lincoln's orders to select "some suitable person" who would be accurate and reliable. Scott endorsed the mission, saying, "It may do good, and can do no harm. It commits no one."

Fox left Washington on the 19th and arrived in Charleston two days later. He went directly to Sumter; Pickens, who gave his permission for the visit, sent along Captain Hartstene of his staff to keep an eye on Fox. Even so, Fox and Anderson managed to evade Hartstene long enough to hold a private conversation. Anderson told Fox that he thought it late for a reinforcement attempt to be made through the harbor; it was too heavily guarded and armed. He warned Fox that if word should leak that reinforcements were on the way, civil war would break out within the hour. Fox, accompanied by Hartstene, returned to Charleston and started back for Washington. Hartstene was then questioned by Beauregard.

"Were you with Captain Fox all the time of his visit?" he asked.

"All but a short period when he was with Major Anderson."

Beauregard looked grim. "I fear we shall have occasion to regret that short visit," he said. He was certain now that Anderson was expecting reinforcements and was preparing to defend the ships when they came in.

Fox saw Lincoln back in Washington on March 23. He still would stick by his original plan with the details slightly altered, he said firmly, despite Anderson's skepticism. But if Lincoln were to act, it should be soon because Anderson was down to "his last slab of bacon and last cup of flour." Lincoln asked Fox to submit a memorandum on his plan, making explicit just how many ships and men would be necessary to implement it. Fox reported as follows:

> Steamers *Pocahontas* at Norfolk, *Pawnee* at Washington, *Harriet Lane* at New York, to be under sailing orders for sea with stores, etc., for one month. Three hundred men to be kept ready for departure from on board the receiving ships at New York. Supplies for twelve months for one hundred men to be put in portable shape, ready for instant shipping. Two hundred men to be ready to leave Governors Island in New York. A large steamer and three tugs conditionally engaged.

Lincoln's private envoy, whose confidential trip south overlapped with Fox's, was his old and close friend, his former law partner, Colonel Ward Hill Lamon. Lamon was neither discreet nor wise, but he had Lincoln's trust (even though, four years later, Lincoln would disregard his pleas not to make public appearances at night). The President could not know that on this mission the colonel, large with self-importance, would cause both North and South some confusion and embarrassment.

Lamon registered at the Charleston Hotel as a Virginian around March 23; his ostensible business was with the postal service. While waiting for an interview with Governor Pickens, an appointment which Lincoln had not authorized him to make, Lamon was accosted by a bellicose gentleman wearing a red bandanna around his neck and a fork-tailed coat. The man, obviously spoiling for a fight, kicked a rope from a corner to the middle of the Charleston Hotel's reading room and demanded, "Do you think that—" he nodded at the rope—"is strong enough to hang a damned Lincoln abolition hireling?"

Lamon, broadcasting his "confidential" mission, answered him with a dignity he hardly deserved. "Sir, I am a Virginian by birth, and a gentleman, I hope, by education and instinct. I was sent here by the President of the United States to see your Governor."

Lamon was rudely interrupted by one of the crowd who had gathered in the reading room: "Damn your President," he shouted.

It was at this moment that former Congressman Lawrence Keitt, who happened to be in the hotel, stopped the incident. He went up to Lamon and told him he was glad to see him there. The heckler in the crowd cried, "Keitt, do you speak to that Lincoln hireling?"

"Stop," roared Keitt in answer. "You insult Lamon, and you insult me! He is a gentleman and my friend. Come, Lamon, let's get us a drink."

The two went to the bar to cool off.

When Lamon finally got in to see Pickens he told the Governor an unauthorized untruth. As a confidential agent, he said, he was in Charleston solely to arrange for the removal of Anderson's garrison. Pickens was delighted to assign Lamon a steamer under a flag of truce for the trip to Sumter.

On March 25, Lamon saw Anderson, and again,

on his own, implied that the entire garrison was to be withdrawn. In fact, the men even began to get their belongings together and pack in preparation. During Lamon's visit to the fort, the batteries at Fort Moultrie blazed away in a meaningful display of gunnery practice. After Lamon had seen Anderson he went back to Pickens and asked if the Governor would let a warship enter the harbor to remove the men from Sumter. "No war vessel will be allowed to enter on any terms" was the Governor's answer.

Lamon had given Anderson and his garrison a false impression; now he left Pickens with one. The garrison, he promised, would be removed in a merchant steamer if a warship was unacceptable to the Governor. Having completely disregarded his instructions simply to observe and report, Lamon left. In Washington on the 27th he had only one fact to report which could be of help to the President: Anderson's food supply would give out by April 15.

While Lamon was away, Lincoln himself set about collecting facts about Anderson and paid a call on Mrs. Abner Doubleday. The wife of Sumter's second-in-command was visiting in Washington and was much surprised when the President was announced in person. Lincoln asked Mrs. Doubleday if she would mind letting him see all the letters she had received from her husband. The President, still trying to cover all possible angles of a situation which was not wholly clear to him, pored over their contents for a long while.

After a Cabinet dinner and secret session on March 28, Lincoln stayed up all night attempting to resolve the problem of Sumter, its relief and the possible consequences. By noon the next day he was certain of what he had to do. He called another Cab-

inet meeting and for form's sake he asked for a vote
on the question. Four members balloted to relieve Sumter; three were against. The opinion of the Cabinet
had unaccountably shifted; and Lincoln's private Secretary, John G. Nicolay, could only describe it as "a
change of sentiment."

Lincoln read aloud Fox's memorandum and endorsed it with a written order to the Secretary of War:
"I desire that an expedition, to move by sea, be got
ready to sail as early as the 6th of April next, the
whole according to the memorandum attached, and that
you co-operate with the Secretary of the Navy for that
object."

On March 30, Captain Fox left for New York
with orders from Lincoln in his pocket:

> You will take charge of the transports in New
> York, having troops and supplies on board, and
> endeavor to deliver the subsistence. If you are op-
> posed in this, you are directed to report the fact to
> the Senior Naval Officer, who will be instructed
> by the Secretary of the Navy to use his entire
> force to open a passage when you will, if possible,
> effect an entrance and place both troops and sup-
> plies in Fort Sumter.

Fox's orders also specified that the expedition was
to rendezvous ten miles east of Charleston Harbor on
the morning of April 11.

The Secretary of the Navy, Gideon Welles, issued orders for the readying of the expedition, including the fitting out of the frigate *Powhatan,* lying at
her berth at the Navy Yard in New York. This ship
was to be the armed escort and carry the launches on
which Fox's scheme largely depended. But now Sew-

ard intervened. Contemptuous of Lincoln's ability to
guide the country through a time of trial, certain that
he himself was destined to be the savior of the Union, Seward remained stubbornly certain that Anderson should be withdrawn and not reinforced. He convinced Lincoln to detach the *Powhatan* from the Sumter expedition and to assign her instead to the relief
of Fort Pickens at Pensacola. Fox was not told of the
change of plan and set out still expecting that the
Powhatan would join the fleet off the South Carolina
coast. After a confusion of telegraphed orders and
counterorders, the frigate left New York on April 6,
but Charleston was not her destination.

A curious exchange, symptomatic of the rumors
and fears that circled Sumter and the despondency
which had lodged in Anderson's mind, took place between Anderson and an unnamed friend of his some-
time after Lamon's visit to the fort. The friend
wrote to Anderson that he had heard from Lamon
that Anderson was planning to blow up Fort Sumter. Anderson wrote back:

> I do not, of course, know what terms Colonel
> Lamon used in repeating the declaration referred
> to. So great was the excitement against this com-
> mand, when I came into this fort, and for weeks
> afterwards, that I was satisfied that, if attacked
> and overcome, not a soul would have been left
> alive and I did, during that time, say more than
> once that, rather than let my garrison suffer that
> fate, I would blow up the fort as they entered into
> the walls, and all who might be in it.
>
> I told Colonel Lamon that I had made that re-
> mark. Cut off from all intercourse with my Gov-
> ernment, I have been compelled to act according

to the dictates of my own judgment, and had the contingencies referred to arisen I should, after prayerfully appealing to God to teach me my duty, have cheerfully and promptly performed it.

I have tried to perform all my duties and I trust I have, by the blessing of God, so acted that the most searching investigation shall show that I have done nothing amiss.

"My hands are tied by my orders"

Still, there was nothing for Anderson to do but wait and worry, hope for help, and watch his enemies prepare a massive assault weapon. The morale in the garrison stayed very low. It was not a glorious time for those inside the walls of Sumter.

Outside, optimism was supreme. Though Anderson occupied the prize possession in the harbor, Pickens and Beauregard were certain it would soon fall to them. They had everything on their side: all the other forts and installations; an enthusiastic local citizenry eager for the call to action; the wholehearted backing of an aggressive Confederate Government; and a pervading spirit of confidence.

Pickens had agents in Washington who reported to him periodically. One of these was Judge John A. Campbell, whose rosy dispatches throughout March did wonders for the Governor's expectations. "I feel perfect confidence," Campbell wrote, "in the fact that Fort Sumter will be evacuated in the next five days."

This message was dated March 15; on the 21st another false lead from the judge: "Fort Sumter is to be evacuated." In anticipation of the great event, Pickens and Beauregard were already trying to decide what terms they would force on Anderson when the time came for him to abandon Sumter.

Then, on the 1st of April, came a disturbing telegram from another agent in Washington, Martin J. Crawford: "I am authorized to say this Government will not undertake to supply Sumter without notice to you." This was accurate, based on reports of Cabinet meetings, which, despite all attempts, never managed to be secret. It was a heavy blow to Pickens and Beauregard, who had chosen to believe Campbell's more palatable dispatches; they were once again faced with the possibility of a show of violence.

On April 3 Anderson had five days' supply of bread left. Again he urgently requested instructions from Washington. But at three o'clock that afternoon another emergency took the major's mind off the food situation. The episode began with heavy fire from the direction of the Southern batteries covering the harbor entrance. The garrison rushed to Sumter's parapet for a good look. They could just make out a small schooner, obviously trying to enter, and the Southern batteries trying to keep her out. Two shots were fired across her bow as she passed Morris Island. The schooner hove to at once and ran up the American flag. Then all batteries let loose in a noisy and impressive show of strength; all the shots went wild except one, which passed through the schooner's mainsail above the boom. Without hesitation she lowered the flag, sailed out past the bar and there dropped anchor.

This was what everyone had been waiting for. Anderson's men responded instantly to the long roll calling them to battle stations. Lieutenant Davis reported to his commander that his battery was ready, its guns shotted, its men eager to begin what they were certain was the battle for Fort Sumter. Should they fire?

Again, Anderson refused to make a split-second decision. Again, he called his officers together for a conference. Five of them favored immediate action with cannon fire. Three of his more cautious officers suggested they try to find out a little more about the mysterious schooner and the Southern cannonade before they took any such drastic action themselves.

Anderson, remembering his February 23 orders from Holt to "avoid collision," sided with the cautious and sent two of his officers to Morris Island in a boat carrying a white flag. The commander of the battery, Colonel De Saussure, met them as they disembarked. He was carrying out orders, he explained, to fire on any ship entering the harbor carrying the flag of the United States. The two officers next rowed out to the schooner. As they approached her they made out her name: *Rhoda B. Shannon*. Aboard, they learned she was out of Boston, bound for Savannah with a cargo of nothing more menacing than ice. Her captain had mistaken Charleston Harbor for Savannah, an error that incredibly cost him no more than a torn sail. The *Shannon*'s bumbling entrance only served to show how trigger-happy Beauregard's batteries were—and how bad their aim was.

But even this serio-comic episode had explosive connotations, Anderson realized. The next day, April 4, Anderson sent off an official report to Washington. His messenger was Lieutenant Talbot, who had already received orders to return to Washington for reassignment and promotion to a captaincy. Accompanied by Snyder, Talbot went to Charleston and saw Pickens, who assured the men that his batteries had been ordered to cease all further random fire. According to his reports from Washington, Pickens told them, Lincoln was going to let Sumter be starved out; Snyder told Anderson this gloomy news immediately on his return to Sumter.

Pickens was not at all sure that Talbot should be allowed to leave Charleston, but Beauregard finally prevailed. Whether or not Talbot reported the *Shannon* incident accurately in Washington, the general argued, it would be all to the good to allow the number of officers at Sumter to be reduced. Talbot left for the capital.

The text of Anderson's message, carried by Talbot to Colonel Lorenzo Thomas, reflected his frustration and bewilderment at a situation which was daily growing graver. It said in part: "The remarks made to me by Colonel Lamon, taken in connection with the tenor of newspaper articles, have induced me to believe that orders would soon be issued for my abandoning this work." Following this statement was his reason for not firing to protect the *Shannon:* he was acting, he said, in strict accordance with the spirit and wording of orders he had received from the War Department, dated February 23. He went on to deplore the fact that "in hourly expectation of receiving definite instructions from the War Department, and with orders so explicit and peremptory as those I am acting under, I deeply regret I did not feel myself at liberty to resent the insult thus offered to the flag of my beloved country." He charged Pickens with the responsibility for what happened: "The authorities here are

certainly blamable for not having constantly sent vessels off to communicate instructions to those seeking
entrance into his harbor." Finally, Talbot's mission:
"I send him on with these despatches, to give the Department the opportunity if deemed proper, to modify,
in consequence of this unfortunate affair, any order
they may have sent to me. I will delay obedience
thereto until I have time to receive a telegram after
Captain Talbot's having reported to the War Department."

During the next few days, Anderson was the victim
of harrying tactics on the part of Pickens. The daily
mail boat from Fort Johnson to Sumter was forced by
the Governor to fly a white flag. Then a mortar battery, presumably in practice firing, exploded a couple
of shells uncomfortably close to Sumter. Pickens and
Beauregard professed ignorance of the near hit, but
Anderson was so outraged by this flagrant game that
he reported the incident to Washington and urged that
"the sooner we are out of this harbor, the better. Our
flag runs an hourly risk of being insulted, and my
hands are tied by my orders; and if this was not the
case, I still have not the *power* to protect it."

If the men at Sumter were not prisoners in name,
they were prisoners in fact. A marked depression settled on the officers and was quickly communicated to the
men under them.

All this changed on the morning of April 7 when
the mail brought a letter from Lincoln to Major Robert Anderson. The letter informed Anderson that an
expedition was on its way to the fort—not to remove
but to reinforce the men. Lincoln's instructions to Anderson, though actually signed by Simon Cameron, the
Secretary of War, carried the President's deep aware-

ness of the momentous news he was sending the men
at Sumter:

> You will therefore hold out, if possible, till the
> arrival of the expedition. It is not, however, the
> intention of the President to subject your com-
> mand to any danger or hardship beyond what, in
> your judgment, would be usual in military life;
> and he has entire confidence that you will act as be-
> comes a patriot and soldier, under all circum-
> stances.
>
> Whenever, if at all, in your judgment, to save
> yourself and your command, a capitulation be-
> comes a necessity, you are authorized to make it.

Anderson had now received the definite information
from Washington he had so long awaited. His reaction was one of surprise that he was to be reinforced
rather than withdrawn, and he was deeply troubled.
His answer to Cameron, which he addressed to Colonel
Lorenzo Thomas, never reached Washington; for later
that same day he received notice from Beauregard that
until further instructions came from the Confederate
Government at Montgomery, the mails to and from
Sumter would be stopped. Only private letters would be
allowed into the fort; all official mail would go to
Montgomery.

On the evening of April 8, Pickens received an emissary from the State Department, Robert S. Chew.
Chew, who was accompanied by Captain Talbot, came
right to the point. "I am directed," he said in a formal tone, "by the President of the United States, to
notify you that an attempt will be made to supply
Fort Sumter with provisions only, and that, if such an
attempt be not resisted, no effort to throw in men,

arms, or ammunition will be made without further notice or except in case of an attack upon the fort."

Here was the bad news Crawford's telegram had
prophesied. Pickens sent for Beauregard, repeated the
message to him, and asked Chew if he would carry a
reply back to Washington. "I have no instructions to
receive a reply," Chew answered stiffly, making it quite
evident that, unlike Buchanan, Lincoln was not willing
to listen to pleas or promises. In retaliation, Pickens
refused to let Captain Talbot communicate with Anderson at the fort.

A crowd had gathered in the short time Chew had
been with Pickens inside the Charleston Hotel. It was
necessary to spirit Chew and Talbot from the hotel in a
carriage with an escort and one of the Governor's
aides. One of the guards remained with them at the
railroad station until they were safely aboard the
train. Meanwhile, an aroused Beauregard had sent
warning messages to stations along the route to Washington asking that copies of all telegrams sent by
Chew be made and wired back to Charleston.

On the morning of April 9 Pickens began the inspection of Anderson's mail. General Beauregard and
Judge Magrath were with him in his office in the
Charleston Hotel. Before them on a table, mesmeriz-
ing and incriminating, lay the bag of mail comman-
deered from the postmaster after it had come from
Sumter. Pickens asked the judge to examine the contents of the mailbag.

"No," he said unexpectedly. "I have too recently
been a United States Judge. I have been in the habit of
sentencing people to the penitentiary for this sort of
thing. So, Governor, let General Beauregard open
them."

Beauregard sidestepped the odious task by flattery. "Certainly not, Governor," he said. "You are the proper person to open these letters."

Pickens was clearly surprised at the reaction of his two principal subordinates. He could not shrink, however, in front of them. "Well," he said, "if you are all so fastidious about it, give them to me." Beauregard pushed the bag over to him.

The Governor was nervous as he opened the first "official" letter from Anderson. It turned out to be to his wife, and Pickens resealed it.

The next document made the unwholesome venture worth while. It was the letter from Anderson to Colonel Lorenzo Thomas dated April 8. It revealed Anderson's utter confusion: first Captain Fox had told him an expedition would probably come to bring him provisions. Then Colonel Lamon had left him with the impression that the garrison would be removed. Then, from Snyder, he had learned of Crawford's telegram to Pickens—and believed it. Now he had Simon Cameron's message from the President telling him to expect the expedition that Fox had hinted at. "I trust that this matter will be at once put in a correct light, as a movement made now, when the South has been erroneously informed that none such will be attempted" (he was obviously not aware, as yet, of Chew's visit to Pickens) "would produce most disastrous results throughout the country. I ought to have been informed that this expedition was to come. . . . We shall strive to do our duty, though I frankly say that my heart is not in the war which I see is to be thus commenced. That God will still avert it, and cause us to resort to pacific measures to maintain our rights, is my ardent prayer."

Pickens immediately telegraphed President Davis in Montgomery. A state of war, he said, had been "inaugurated by the authorities in Washington. All information of a public nature is absolutely necessary to the Confederate cause. You will see by these letters how it is intended to supply the fort."

Now the Confederate military was rapidly gaining strength. The State Secretary called out 5,000 men, and the Confederate Secretary of War recommended calling up 3,000 volunteers from Louisiana, Texas, Alabama and Mississippi. The garrisons on Morris Island were enlarged to 2,100 men, and ten companies of 800 men and two regiments were due on April 10. The forts facing Sumter contained 3,700 men, ready at their battle stations. Pickens placed a rifle regiment, two Dahlgren guns, four 24-pounders in battery, and forty separate riflemen on the lower end of Morris Island to prevent a landing.

And on Sumter, Anderson drove his men without let-up on the final readying of the fort's weapons. Last-minute adjustments were made. All gun carriages not in use were broken up for timber. It was a gallant last effort, and it elated the men whose long inactivity and constant waiting would now soon come to an end.

"It is now generally understood that an actual conflict is likely to take place in the harbor of Charleston before the end of the week," the New York *Herald* commented. "This prospect naturally depresses all kinds of property. The Market looks very blue."

CHAPTER
THIRTEEN

"He would not consent"

Four hundred and twenty-five miles from Charleston Harbor, in a large brick building that came to be known as "Jeff Davis' State Department," the new President of the Confederate States sat down with seven members of his Cabinet to discuss a crucial telegram from Beauregard, sent the night before. The wire read: "An authorized messenger from President Lincoln just informed Governor Pickens and myself that provisions will be sent to Fort Sumter peaceably or otherwise by force."

The men who had to deal with this bit of intelligence were oddly lacking in the qualifications for the jobs they had been honored with. The Secretary of War, Leroy Pope Walker, had no experience whatever in military affairs. German-born Christopher Memminger, Secretary of the Treasury, was a good lawyer and politician—but not especially knowledgeable

about financial matters. Davis had chosen Stephen R.
Mallory to be his Navy Secretary; "for a landsman
he has much knowledge of nautical affairs"—thus
Davis justified his selection. So far his department was
mythical, as the Confederate Navy had no ships. The
Postmaster General was a former Indian fighter, a
huge brute of a man named John R. Reagan whose
colleagues never invited him or his wife to their social
gatherings because they considered him too much a rus-
tic. The Vice President was dwarfish, sickly Alexander
Hamilton Stephens, who was reluctant, as he had once
said, to "strike the first blow" and who mistrusted
the others. And Howell Cobb, the appropriately
pompous President of the Confederate Congress, was
really more a soldier than statesman and in fact re-
nounced politics for the battlefield during the war. Secretary of State Robert Toombs, who joined the others
after the session began that morning, was opinionated
and often violent in language and sentiment—not the
best qualities for an office which requires tact and diplomacy. The only man truly suited for his job was the
lawyer Judah P. Benjamin, whom Davis had made his
Attorney General. Benjamin was a fast-talking oppor-
tunist who had once nearly fought a duel with his
present chief and who epitomized the most stoutly pro-
slave sympathizer. A tragicomic note on the Secretary
of War, Mr. Walker, is that he did not believe in violence and had promised to "wipe up with his handkerchief every drop of blood spilled." And President
Davis himself was really yearning to be a great soldier
in the field and win military glory and immortality
for himself.

The prevailing sentiment behind the whitewashed

doors of the meeting room was of hurt and bewilderment, as much as anger. The men felt betrayed by
Lincoln, yet they did not understand his tactics; a
number of them had been sure that, like his predecessor,
Lincoln would not take decisive action against them.

Davis was for immediate action and had drafted a
strong telegram to Beauregard which the Cabinet was
considering when Secretary of State Toombs entered
the room. This volatile man was handed Davis' answer;
he read it and reacted with uncharacteristic caution.
"This will inaugurate a civil war greater than
any the world has yet seen," he said. "It will lose us
every friend in the North. It puts us in the wrong. It
is fatal. I do not feel competent to advise you."

If all the men present had not been under the influence of the aggressive Jeff Davis, if they did not feel,
moreover, that it was time to take a definite stand, and
if they had not been certain war was inevitable, they
might have cheered Toombs's surprisingly tolerant
tone. But the men of the Cabinet knew there was no
turning around now; and they were willing to forego
their misgivings for the sake of their President, a man
dedicated to his cause. The Cabinet overruled the Secretary of State and approved the wire to Beauregard.

The telegram, signed by Davis, said: "If you have
no doubt of the authorized character of the agent who
communicated to you the intention of the Washington
Government to supply Fort Sumter by force, you will
at once demand its evacuation and if this is refused,
proceed in such manner as you may determine to reduce it. Answer."

Beauregard answered: "Ought not demand of
Sumter be made also by Commissioners at Washington

for its evacuation?" The general apparently disliked having the buck passed to him; he tried to hand it right back to his Government.

Secretary of War Walker would not accept this evasion. He wired on April 10: "Unless there are special reasons connected with your own condition it is considered proper that you should make the demand at an early hour." Again Beauregard wired to Montgomery. He needed another twenty-four hours, he said. The prelude to the Civil War was being played on telegraph wires.

On April 1 Beauregard had optimistically informed the Cabinet that his batteries were almost ready for action. But now, nine days later, he was still not prepared in two crucial areas, one no less vital than the other. For one, he did not have the necessary ammunition for a prolonged bombardment; the powder on hand could be stretched to last three hours at most. Beauregard expected a shipment of powder daily, but until it arrived he could not, he felt, risk opening any action. Then, he knew that his gunners were inexperienced and might easily panic at the sight of a Federal fleet cannonading its way into Charleston Harbor. He was fairly certain that they would not stand a chance against a naval attack, especially if aided by the guns of Sumter; he began to feel that maybe they ought to hold off. Captain Hartstene, Beauregard's Chief of Naval Operations, had notified him that "Sumter *can* be relieved, by boats from vessels outside of the bars, on any night as dark as the last. If a vessel of war is placed off each bar, when Sumter opens fire I will lose all my steamers for there will be no escape for me." Hartstene had substantiated Beauregard's initial reluctance with hard and unpleasant fact.

But the Creole general was a good soldier, and he wired again to Montgomery that he would obey and ask for Anderson's evacuation "tomorrow at twelve o'clock."

On April 10 the Charleston *Mercury* came out with a dramatic announcement, full of high-sounding righteousness and hope:

> The gage is thrown down and we accept the challenge. We will meet the invader and the God of battles must decide the issue between the hostile hirelings of abolition, hate and Northern tyranny, and the people of South Carolina defending their freedom and their homes. We hope such a blow will be struck on behalf of the South, that Sumter and Charleston Harbor will be remembered by the North as long as they exist as a people.

Along about seven o'clock that night rain began to fall on Charleston. It soon grew denser and violent; a thunderstorm broke, drenching the men on watch at Sumter as they peered anxiously around the harbor, illumined now and again by flashes of lightning. Anderson and his officers made their round of inspection after a meal of salt pork, rice, crackers from the bottom of the barrel, and water. The last drops of oil were in the lanterns they carried with them along the gloomy, dank galleries and deserted parade. By ten o'clock the thunder and lightning stopped but the rain continued in a steady downpour.

Just before midnight two Confederate tugboats without running lights slipped through the dark channel and towed the monstrous floating battery behind them to its anchorage off Sullivan's Island. They made the trip undetected.

With the twelfth stroke of the clock seven guns at Citadel Green in the city of Charleston boomed simultaneously. It was the signal for the 17th Regiment, South Carolina Volunteers, to muster. Soon the wet misty streets of the old city were filled with men running to their posts, making their way down to the Battery where boats were docked, waiting for them.

By 3:00 A.M. on April 11 the 17th Regiment was ready for action at the Morris Island fortifications. By 3:30 four regiments of a thousand men each went into bivouac on Charleston Green, waiting for orders from their commander, Colonel Rion. Excitement mounted throughout the night and into the morning. The city was pulsing to drum rolls and the sound of marching feet. Uniformed volunteers shouldered the unaccustomed heaviness of recently issued muskets and met their companies at almost every street corner and public square; there were not enough armories in the city to accommodate all the men who wanted to fight.

Surgeon General Gibbs made last-minute preparations to receive the wounded. Ambulances harnessed to teams of horses stood grimly outside the hospital. Old men in the Home Guard joined the general call to arms as couriers, going about through the city tugging on doorpulls, arousing all to the emergency, long anticipated, excitingly sudden. No one, it seemed, wanted to be exempt. Merchants, lawyers, preachers, students, clerks, ordinary laborers poured out of their homes and stood in rank together. "The affairs in this city are culminating to a point," wired the Charleston correspondent of the New York *Herald,* understating it. "The greatest enthusiasm prevails among all classes."

And two men, nearing seventy—Edmund Ruffin, a Virginia planter, and Louis Wigfall, the former U.S. Senator from Texas, a native of South Carolina who had returned to Charleston because he could not bear to miss the opening gun—strapped on swords and joined the "Army."

It was a time for elation. No blood had yet been shed; honor and glory and victory still seemed attainable.

As Surgeon Crawford took over the watch on the parapet at Sumter he sensed something of spring in the westerly breeze which freshened as the sun rose. It promised to be a clear, sparkling April morning bringing relief from a hard winter. All during the time he stood there, unusually heavy activity churned the harbor waters; sloops, ferries, guard boats, schooners—all manner of craft—moved purposefully through the channels, signaling constantly to the batteries surrounding Fort Sumter and carrying Confederate troops to their posts.

Crawford took it all in with some apprehension.

When he in turn was relieved by the sentry he went below to one of the batteries, where he found Anderson pacing, deep in thought, near his big guns. Crawford thought him greatly depressed. "He seemed to realize," the doctor noted later, "that upon himself rested mainly the great responsibility. He had endeavored to avert the crisis by every means in his power; he had failed and the struggle was unavoidable and imminent. His sense of duty now overcame every other consideration, and he was prepared to meet the worst." It is not difficult to imagine what this Southern major, trapped in the most crucial military command of his generation, was undergoing.

More boats, large and small, passed the fort, coming close, as if daring the Federal soldiers to fire at them. As the sky brightened, the dreaded floating battery was discovered firmly beached in position on the upper end of Sullivan's Island, protected behind the breakwater. Anderson remarked on it coolly: "It is admirably placed for pouring a murderous fire on us." Now Fort Sumter was truly surrounded.

This last bit of war machinery did not especially disturb the men. "The greatest enthusiasm prevailed among them," Surgeon Crawford wrote later. "While their long confinement was telling on them, they were yet in good spirits, although unfit for fatiguing labor."

At 6:30 the fort's drummer beat assembly and the entire garrison, with the exception of those who had been standing the night watch, formed in rank on the open parade for roll call. When all were accounted for, the men filed below for breakfast: a strip of salt pork each, stale rice, broken crackers, water. Anderson ate the same meal as his men. What was left of the cracker crumbs was carefully scraped together to be mixed with the remainder of rice and salt pork, for the evening meal. The food stock was now down to several barrels of pork, half a barrel of salt. Bread and flour were gone. The rice supply, which had survived rainstorm and shattered glass, was now nearly exhausted. The major had figured that provisions could not last past April 15. He knew that Lincoln's promised relief expedition would have to arrive by that date or he would have to give up.

After breakfast Anderson ordered every man to gather up his belongings and bedding and move into the gun casemates for safety. He instructed the men to round up all the fort's surplus blankets, uniforms and bedding from the hospital to be cut up and sewn into cartridge bags. This would bring the count of bags, ready-made and makeshift, up to 700.

While the cartridge bags were being readied, another detail of men distributed ammunition to the gun rooms all over the fort. The long tedium of inactivity over, the half-starved men moved with speed and efficiency, the promise of action propelling and animating them.

Anderson assigned his officers to their battle stations: Doubleday to the battery of two 32-pounders in the right gorge angle on the lower tier which bore upon the batteries at Cummings Point; Lieutenant Jeff C. Davis to the batteries on Doubleday's left; Surgeon Crawford not to the hospital but to the three 32-pounders on the western face of the fort bearing directly on the floating battery and covering, at the same time, the Dahlgren mounted on the beach below at Sullivan's Island.

Those whose tasks were finished rushed to the parapets, where they stood looking anxiously seaward or watching the Confederates at work on the fortifications.

In Charleston, Colonel A. R. Chisholm left his quarters in answer to a summons from General Beauregard. When Beauregard assumed command in March, Chisholm, a prosperous planter, had gone to the Governor and requested that he be made the general's aide. He knew the harbor, and he had a six-oared barge and a crew to man it, which were at the Governor's disposal, free of charge. Pickens made him lieutenant colonel and aide to Beauregard on the spot.

In this role, Chisholm had, on several occasions, visited Fort Sumter. He must have been an amiable gentleman, for he struck up a friendship with Ander-

son and some of the officers. On one occasion, coming
under a flag of truce and with Beauregard's approval,
he brought along a few cases of claret and some cigars
for Anderson, who had, on the colonel's previous visit,
complained in jest that he had run out of luxuries.

At about noon, when Chisholm reached headquarters,
Colonel James Chesnut and Captain Stephen Lee, late
of the U.S. Army, were there waiting for him. To
these three Beauregard entrusted the delivery of the
surrender ultimatum to Anderson. Shortly thereafter,
the colonel's six-oared barge pulled away from the
Charleston wharf and headed toward Sumter. As soon
as it had left, Beauregard wired to Secretary of War
Walker in Montgomery: "Demand sent at 2. Allowed
until 6 to answer."

The three officers reached Fort Sumter at 3:30. They
were met formally by Lieutenant Jeff C. Davis, who
escorted them to the guardroom, where Major Anderson greeted them. Colonel Chesnut acted as spokesman. While he was certain, he said, that an amicable
settlement could be reached, he must demand that Anderson evacuate Fort Sumter at once. He read the proposed surrender terms:

> All proper facilities will be afforded for the re-
> moval of yourself and command together with
> company arms and property, and all private prop-
> erty to any post in the United States you may
> select. The flag which you have upheld so long and
> with so much fortitude under the most trying cir-
> cumstances, may be saluted by you on taking it
> down.

Anderson listened quietly, then summoned his officers, who gathered around him in silence. He read them

Beauregard's note and they discussed it for more than an hour, at the end of which Anderson finally divulged former Secretary Floyd's confidential message of December 1860: "It will be your duty to yield to necessity and make the best terms in your power." The tone and intent of Floyd's message so infuriated Anderson's officers that they reached an immediate decision: They would refuse to abandon the fort.

Anderson drafted a note of refusal for the Confederate officers to bring Beauregard: "General: I have the honor to acknowledge the receipt of your communication demanding the evacuation of the fort and to say in reply thereto, that it is a demand with which I regret that my sense of honor and my obligations to my government, prevent my compliance." Anderson thanked the three for the fair and courteous terms they had proposed.

Anderson personally escorted the emissaries to their boat. Just as they were about to climb aboard Anderson asked, "Will General Beauregard open his batteries without notice to me?"

The Confederate officers seemed hesitant and slightly embarrassed. "I think not," answered Colonel Chesnut, then added, "No, I can say to you he will not, without giving you further notice."

Then Anderson made a curious, unaccountable remark to Chesnut: "I will await the first shot," he said, "and if you do not batter us to pieces, we will be starved out in a few days anyway." The colonel instantly recognized that this information, an inexplicable lapse on Anderson's part, might have some importance to his Government. He asked permission to repeat to his general what Anderson had said. Anderson answered noncommittally, "That is the fact of the case."

Anderson's conduct at this moment is anomalous. Did he hope that Beauregard, informed that the garrison would soon be starved out of Sumter, would prefer to withhold his fire and that the Federal expedition might reach him in time? Was he trying to throw off all responsibility for bloodshed? Was his loyalty wavering, or was his discretion simply undermined by fatigue and illness? He must, at any rate, have been aware how valuable this information would be to Beauregard. The general repeated it verbatim in a telegram to Montgomery which he sent off that afternoon with a request for an answer. An hour later Walker's reply was in his hands:

> Do not desire needlessly to bombard Fort Sumter. If Major Anderson will state the time at which, as indicated by him, he will evacuate and agree that in the meantime he will not use his guns against us unless ours should be employed against Fort Sumter, you are authorized thus to avoid the effusion of blood. If this, or its equivalent, be refused, reduce the fort as your judgment decides to be most practicable.

At 12:15 A.M., April 12, a boat carrying Colonels Chisholm and Chesnut, Captain Lee and Roger Pryor drew up to Fort Sumter. It was a delegation on the second and final round of negotiation for the surrender.

While he made the four officers wait, Anderson called his staff together. When all were assembled, Colonel Chesnut handed Anderson the second note. It read:

If you will state the time at which you will evacuate Fort Sumter and agree that in the meantime
you will not use your guns against us, unless ours
shall be employed against Fort Sumter, we will
abstain from opening fire upon you. Colonel Chesnut and Captain Lee are authorized by me to enter into an agreement with you. You are therefore
requested to communicate to them an open answer.

It was signed by Beauregard.

Anderson realized at once that if he agreed to this
note, he would be bested by the South; unless Sumter
was fired on, he would be prevented from using his
guns to aid the relief expedition he knew was on the
way, while Beauregard could hammer away at the
fleet, unhampered.

The major wanted to stall for time; he kept the
general's messengers at the fort for several hours.
While they waited impatiently, Anderson went into
conference with his officers. He wanted to know pre-
cisely how long the men could go on, with the present
rations unaltered. Surgeon Crawford ventured that
they could hold on for five days altogether—three without food.

At the end of the conference Major Anderson wrote
his answer to Beauregard:

General: I have the honor to acknowledge the
receipt of your second communication and to state
in reply that, cordially uniting with you in the desire to avoid the useless effusion of blood, I will,
if provided with the proper and necessary means
of transportation, evacuate Fort Sumter by noon

of the 15th, and that I will not in the meantime
open my fire upon your force unless compelled to
do so by some hostile act against this fort or the
flag of my Government by the forces under your
command, or by some portion of them, should I
not receive prior to that time controlling instructions from my Government or additional supplies.

When Anderson handed Chesnut his answer to
Beauregard at 3:15, the colonel complained about the
delay. After reading it, he became even more annoyed.
He told Anderson he thought the whole affair now
seemed manifestly futile and that his answer placed the
South at a disadvantage. He did not see how this could
possibly be acceptable to his Government.

Colonel Chesnut then sat down and wrote out his
final notice to Anderson:

Fort Sumter, South Carolina, April 12th, 3:20,
A.M.

Sir: By authority of Brigadier General Beauregard commanding the Provisional forces of the
Confederate States, we have the honor to notify
you that he will open the fire of his batteries on
Fort Sumter in one hour from this time. We have
the honor to be very respectfully, Your obedient
servants, James Chesnut, Jr., Aide-de-Camp,
Stephen D. Lee, Captain, C.S.A., Aide-de-Camp.

Chesnut handed Anderson the note; the major was
visibly affected by it. Again, he personally escorted the
men to the wharf, where he shook hands with them and
said sadly, "If we never meet in this world again,
God grant that we may meet in the next." He seemed,
beneath his determination, beaten already.

As soon as the messengers were away, Anderson ordered his men awakened. He told them, as they stood in rank, to expect an attack any moment. He ordered them not to fire until instructed to do so—that would be at least until daybreak. When the word is given, "You are to fire slowly and carefully."

Chesnut and the others reported back to Beauregard immediately, and the general sent off a wire to Walker in Montgomery: "He would not consent. I write today."

It was obvious to all now that no conceivable human act could alter the course of what had been building up for months. Anderson, as he said goodbye to the four Confederate officers, men to whom he felt far more deeply the friendship that might have united them than the enmity which artificially separated them, could not do more.

CHAPTER
FOURTEEN

"A trifling difference of opinion"

Dark still held Fort Sumter, the harbor and Charleston in suspension. Sounds of unrelieved activity came drifting over the water and penetrated into the casemates where Sumter's men, unable to sleep, waited restlessly for the first light and the first shots. The men sat around talking softly. Some of them must have felt the apprehension of a man about to enter a dark room where an unknown assailant waits in an unknown corner. All expected fire; it had been an uncomfortable and long night.

Charleston, too, was alerted, but there the spirit was not apprehension but expectancy. Even before sunrise men and women crowded down to the Battery for a clean sweeping view of the harbor. They were soon to see Federal ships standing off the bar. As reported on the Charleston *Mercury* bulletin board, these ships were the *Pawnee, Harriet Lane,* and *Baltic* carrying Federal provisions, arms and men.

Shortly before daylight the ships had rendezvoused ten miles east of Charleston. Captain Fox rowed from the *Baltic* to talk to Commander Rowan on board the *Pawnee.* "You are to stand in for the bar immediately with your ship," Fox told him.

Rowan refused: "My orders are to hold the *Pawnee* ten miles east of the light and await the *Powhatan.* I am not going in there to begin civil war!" Neither man knew at the time that the *Powhatan* had been detached from the expedition. Fox returned to the *Baltic,* which, followed by the *Harriet Lane,* began to head cautiously into the channel.

Mrs. Mary Chesnut, conscious always of her little role as an observer of history, sat down again at her escritoire and wrote in her journal: "I do not pretend to sleep. How can I? If Anderson does not accept terms at four the orders are he shall be fired upon. I count four, St. Michael's bells chime out, and I begin to hope"—though she does not say what she hopes for.

At Fort Johnson, at Fort Moultrie, at Cummings Point on Morris Island, each officer in charge paced impatiently, looked at his watch, then at the sky, then toward his men. They saw no signal to begin battle. They waited.

Colonels Chesnut and Chisholm, Captain Lee, and Roger Pryor rowed directly to Fort Johnson after leaving Anderson. Shortly after 4:00 A.M. they landed at Johnson and proceeded to Captain George S. James's quarters. With a keen sense of his role in the scene about to commence, Chesnut gave James the written order to open fire. Immediately the fort's men were aroused and at their battle stations. Captain James

then turned to Roger Pryor and said in a voice husky
with generosity and a sense of the moment, "You are
the only man to whom I would give up the honor of
firing the first gun of the war." Pryor shook his
head, obviously much moved. "I could not fire the
first guns," he replied, relinquishing the honor. Captain Lee later recalled that Pryor's manner seemed as
sepulchral as Major Anderson's had been not an hour
previously.

Chisholm and Pryor stayed at Fort Johnson. Colonel Chesnut and Captain Lee, however, decided to
row out into the harbor for a grandstand seat to the
battle. They rowed to a point somewhat less than
halfway to Sumter and there shipped oars, sat back
and waited, their boat drifting in the tide. Fort Sumter still seemed to them no more than a great hulking
shape rising out of the water: it might have been a
rock or a sea monster.

The bells of St. Michael's sounded again. It was
now 4:30. Captain James checked his watch, stepped
smartly to his battery and grasped the lanyard of a
ten-inch mortar.

The first shot of the Civil War went roaring into
the air, flew over the water, and burst, a perfect hit,
on the deserted parade of Fort Sumter. Charleston
tradition has it that Edmund Ruffin, the sixty-seven-
year-old Virginia planter who attached himself to the
South Carolina cause, fired the first shot at Fort
Sumter. But both Captain Lee and General Beauregard attest to James's priority. Ruffin, who, despondent
that the South had lost its war for independence, four
years later committed suicide, probably did fire the
second gun from a battery on Sullivan's Island. And
then, wrote the amateur historian, Captain Chester,

"the batteries opened on all sides and shot and shell went screaming over Sumter as if an army of devils were whooping it up."

The vigilant Mrs. Chesnut, whose husband was drifting around the harbor in a small open boat, fell to her knees with the first shot and prayed, threw a shawl over her shoulders, and went up to the roof of her house to watch the fight. Governor Pickens surveyed the scene with a telescope from the roof of General Beauregard's headquarters in town.

At first, the garrison at Sumter was so struck by the novelty of being fired on that the men stood out on the parapets, watching the shells coming over too high. But soon they retired to the safety of the bomb shelters to wait for the call to action.

When the bombardment started Captain Doubleday was dozing on a cot in the magazine of the fort nearest Morris Island. He had been awakened at four by his commander and had been able to return to an uneasy sleep. Suddenly a shell exploded near the captain's head, leaving a gaping hole in the magazine wall and setting some loose powder on fire. Doubleday sprang off the cot, took a look at the room which was rapidly filling with smoke, and rushed outside, expecting to be blown to bits—but there was no explosion. And so the last man asleep at Sumter was catapulted from his rest.

Until daylight, the situation changed very little. Anderson had as yet not fired a single shot from Sumter—a fact which the enemy found puzzling. The Sumter garrison attended roll call as usual and then went below for their breakfast. So far the routine was undisturbed.

By the time the *Baltic* and the *Harriet Lane* had

neared the shoreline, the roar of cannon could be heard distinctly by the men on board. Rowan, despairing of the arrival of the *Powhatan,* had finally brought the *Pawnee* into the channel and, realizing that Anderson was under fire, he had a change of heart. He signaled to Fox that he intended to run past the Confederate batteries, blast his way into Anderson, and, if necessary, share Anderson's fate. Now it was Fox who counseled waiting. He boarded the *Pawnee* once more: "The Government does not expect such gallant sacrifice from you," he told Rowan. Fox's orders to provision Fort Sumter peaceably were obviously no longer in force, and he felt that a daylight attempt to reach Anderson would be suicidal.

In the mess hall Doubleday found his fellow officers in a "merry" mood. But the officers' mess boy, a mulatto from Charleston, was completely demoralized by the experience and crouched trembling against the wall. The officers' breakfast menu was varied by the addition of a small ration of farina Surgeon Crawford had discovered in a corner of the hospital.

By 7:00 A.M. Anderson started planning and moving. He knew that most of the enemies' fortifications were well protected by earthworks, iron plating, timbers, sandbags, lunettes and shutters which were raised to permit a shot to be fired, then directly lowered to protect the weapon. Where and how best to penetrate the armor was his immedate problem. He decided that since the Confederate mortars could hurl shells to burst over his gunners on the barbette, he would open action with the casemate guns which were shielded.

Anderson ordered Doubleday to divide his company into three details whose targets were two installations on Morris Island and one on Sullivan's Island respectively. Doubleday took charge of the first battery, Lieutenant Davis the second, and Sergeant James Carmody, known as the "wild Irishman," the third.

Doubleday fired the first Federal shot at 7:30. The 32-pound shells struck the ironclad battery on Cummings Point on Morris Island but bounced off the shield like rubber balls. The battery answered him with three 8-inch columbiads which scored three hits and scattered Federal masonry in all directions. They continued to duel, killing or injuring no one but using up indiscriminate quantities of ammunition.

Sergeant Carmody relinquished his command to Surgeon Crawford when the noncombatant volunteered his services to Anderson. Crawford, a vigorous fighter, eager for glory as a soldier rather than as a healer, (in fact he soon resigned his medical commission for a purely military one), opened fire on Moultrie, which, in turn, showered Sumter with a steady fire of huge mortar shells, burying themselves in the parade's sand, their explosions shaking the fort like an earthquake's tremor.

Crawford's battery also aimed for the menacing floating battery, but the shells continued to bounce harmlessly off its iron roof. Crawford, realizing that he was doing no damage to the enemy, requested and got permission from Anderson to move his command to a more advantageous position.

The fire that had started when shells struck the magazine was by this time sending smoke and powder fumes throughout the fort and into the casemates, where ventilation was already poor. Added to this smoking confusion were clouds of dust thrown up and scattered by bricks which had been hit and disintegrated.

It was time for Anderson to make his rounds of the batteries in action. He discovered that his prebattle figure of 700 cartridges had dwindled to a dangerously low number; his men had not been sparing. And worse yet, there was little to show for it—somehow, he was not disabling the enemy's armament; a shell would strike a Confederate embrasure, Anderson's gunners would congratulate each other on their aim, but the gun they thought they had put out of commission would open fire again. Moultrie was giving them the most trouble.

Chiefly responsible for Moultrie's effectiveness were armaments which Anderson's field glasses did not reveal: 18-foot-thick embrasures and casemates. In addition heavy cotton bales, serving as huge shutters, kept the guns safely covered except at the moment of firing.

Anderson felt he had to try to conserve what little ammunition he had left, so he confined all fire to six of his guns: two bearing on Moultrie, two on Cummings Point, and two on the western end of Sullivan's Island. An occasional shot was fired by Captain Seymour toward Fort Johnson, just to keep the enemy on his toes.

At about 11:00 A.M. Lieutenant Meade stepped up to relieve Crawford, and Captain Seymour to relieve Doubleday. Lack of success did not rout Seymour's sense of humor (perhaps the battle seemed somewhat "stagy" even to those who took part in it—there had been not one fatality or wounded). "Doubleday," Seymour asked, "what in the world is the matter here, and what is all this uproar about?"

"There is a trifling difference of opinion between us and our neighbors opposite," the second-in-command answered, "and we are trying to settle it."

Still the shells flew and burst. For a few happy, free moments Sergeant Carmody slipped up to the parapet against orders and, one by one, fired every gun along the barbette. His singlehanded war with the Confederacy might have had some effect had he been able to reload by himself, for his aim was surprisingly good. Even the few workmen left in the fort got into the spirit and started loading and firing with an expert touch the guns Crawford had abandoned earlier. Anderson gave permission for them to remain at this station.

All day it kept up. The casemates, which had not been penetrated, were in good condition, but fires kept breaking out in the officers' quarters. Each time the flames seemed to be getting out of control, a party of men would have to go down and extinguish them.

Then, with evening, came the rain. Light at first, it soon lashed itself into a fierce storm. Anderson, fearing a landing by the enemy in the dark and rainy night, ordered the men to maintain a twenty-four-hour alert; he stationed one man also in each embrasure. The fleet which had stood outside the harbor since morning, now could not possibly have got close to Sumter—gale winds had transformed the already treacherous waters into a mariner's nightmare—and Anderson expected and received no help from the ships. Still looking for the *Powhatan,* the *Baltic* struck on a shoal but soon freed herself. The thick weather and heavy seas also frustrated at the last moment an attempt to send at least one boat, its crew organized and ready, to Sumter. But despite the storm, mortar shells from Confederate guns streamed through the night sky and plummeted down inside the fort or struck the outside wall, the scarp, or landed on the

parade with fierce flashes of red light and almost ani-
mal-like roars.

Anderson stationed men on the parapet in case they
should be called on to signal the relief ships—which
seemed unlikely. On his rounds with his officers, the
major could see that the enemy was also alert and had
lighted huge piles of wood on the hulks anchored in
the entrance of the inner harbor.

Soon after midnight Surgeon Crawford and Lieutenant Snyder made an official check of actual damage
done to Sumter. They found the walls to be completely
defaced with great holes, especially that part that
faced Moultrie. Occasionally they saw where a solid
shell had penetrated the wall twelve inches, leaving an
ugly wound. The enemy's Blakely rifled gun had been
so healthy a weapon that its shells had buried themselves into the lower end of the embrasure on the right
gorge angle almost two feet—but not far enough, so
massive was Sumter's armor. Crawford and Snyder
also discovered that many of the booby traps had been
set off and killed by enemy fire. But their report was
on the whole good: in spite of this and total damage
to parapet, roof and chimneys, Sumter was still in
working order.

Meanwhile, volunteer troops from all over the
state poured into Charleston like an army of ants.
They came on foot, on horseback, and in every im-
aginable variety of vehicle. Business on the 12th of
April had been suspended and it was reported that five
thousand ladies were ready to respond to the call and
make any sacrifice for their men and state. Men and
women were crammed into every available spot at the
Battery and had been watching all day, many through
glasses. The spectacle was gloriously noisy and re-

mained the chief interest of every citizen. Even the storm did not drive them away from their roofs and railings.

Shortly after midnight, General Beauregard left his Charleston Hotel headquarters for the works on Morris Island.

"Thank God the day has come"

During the night the storm over Sumter waned, then blew out to sea; by dawn of the 13th the sky was quite clear. With the rising sun came intensified fire from the Southern batteries. Anderson's men breakfasted on the usual small rations of salt pork and water, then went to the gun casemates to take up their stations.

Anderson, to conserve what was left of his ammunition, decided to restrict his fire to the installation on Moultrie known as "Sumter Battery" because it was directly opposite and most accurate. Anderson fired a token shot every ten minutes.

The garrison still expected the fleet to come to their aid. It could be glimpsed standing outside the bar but, inexplicably to Anderson and his men, did not make any attempt to enter the harbor. The ships were as little help to the Federal troops as the spectators at Charleston were to the Southern volunteers.

At 8:00 A.M. the Confederate gunners stepped up their fire. The officers' quarters at Sumter was struck again and began to burn. A fire brigade rushed into the interior of the fort with axes and buckets of water to put out the blaze. At 10:00 the same thing happened again. A violent struggle raged between men and flames, which found the woodwork and wooden partitions excellent targets. It became obvious after a while that the flames threatened not only an entire block of the fort but also a magazine where 300 barrels of powder were stored.

While the officers tried to prevent the fire from traveling too fast, a party of soldiers rolled the powder barrels from the magazine to a more sheltered spot and covered them with damp blankets, wrenched from the cots. They had time to rescue only ninety-six barrels before they were forced to close the heavy iron door behind them. Finally Anderson ordered all but three of these to be dumped into the water; the place was turning into a powder keg and he did not want to chance a grand explosion. (The barrels were to bob in the harbor like apples for days.) But the fire raged on, and smoke and cinders eddied through the fort, propelled by a southerly wind. The men stayed at their guns, coughing for fresh air.

Frustrated perhaps by their failure to make any headway against the enemy's guns, two of Doubleday's sergeants decided to see how much of a fuss they could kick up. Along the beach on Sullivan's Island, out of the line of fire, stood a crowd of spectators watching the artillery duel; the two sergeants chose this clump of human beings for their target.

They made their way to two ten-inch columbiads mounted *en barbette* in the casemate, aimed into the crowd and fired. The first shot roared over the heads of the stunned spectators and crashed through Moultrie House, the fashionable summer hotel, fifty yards further on, where, according to the Charleston *Mercury* correspondent, "a party of gentlemen were seated in the parlor watching the fight." The ball entered the second story, flew through the kitchen, "scattering the gentlemen miscellaneously." The next shot neatly sliced off part of Moultrie House's second story. Elated by their small but miraculously non-fatal success, Doubleday's disobedient soldiers fired off a 42-pounder on the parapet which was already loaded and aimed. The shell from this one grazed the crest of Cummings Point's ironclad battery; if the gun had not been aimed too high, they might have put the battery out of commission.

Ordinarily it took six men to throw the big gun back in gear after it was reloaded and the two did not even attempt it; they decided to fire her as she was. By this time the enemy had discovered them and had almost every gun turned on them, throwing a hurricane of shot as they tried to fire again. But one of the sergeants, fearing his own officers' anger, decided he had better have a look to see if the coast was clear. He left his cohort lying safely on the parapet with the lanyard in his hand, and ran down the spiral stairs. He found they were still undiscovered and started up again. Just as he reached the top, the gun, having been fired in the wrong position, came hurtling over backward from the recoil. It plunged by, narrowly missing him. The two sergeants were now thoroughly frightened by what they had done and, swearing each other to everlasting secrecy, they crawled under the disabled gun without looking to see where the last shot had landed. But Captain Chester saw it: it had hit the Iron Battery and half buried it under sand.

It was only a little after 11:00 A.M. and the interior of the fort was a holocaust of flames, smoke, cinders. One fifth of it was now actively burning. Anderson's exhausted gunners, almost suffocated by smoke and sulphur fumes, survived by throwing themselves face down on the floor and covering their mouths and nostrils with wet cloths. The smoke also threatened the firefighters with suffocation, but a lucky change of wind saved them. All the while shells, both their own and the enemy's, were exploding in the burning rooms and every few minutes huge chunks of masonry crashed to the floor with a hideous reverberation, flinging bricks and mortar into the air. Outside, the towers at each angle of the fort, where shells had been stored, were shattered by successive explosions.

The massive wooden gates were crumbling and burning; the wall behind dissolved into a heap of rubble. Windows in the gorge and sally ports had burst open. The Confederate gunners kept hammering away on orders from their officers, who had only to look at the ruin they were making out of Sumter to realize Anderson could not hold out much longer. Sumter's courage and endurance were impressive, and the men in the Confederate forts began to cheer each answer from her guns as it came over and to hoot and catcall at the fleet standing so idly—and so safely—outside the bar. Even the rebels, determined to take Sumter, felt that Anderson should have the support of his own Government's forces.

Around 1:30 the Sumter flagstaff was hit and toppled. Lieutenant Hall, Sergeant Hart and Captain Seymour immediately ran the flag up another staff which they mounted on a gun carriage on the parapet, for the enemy to see and admire. The men, most of them exhausted from fighting fires and dodging flames, walked about as in a daze—but no one talked of quitting.

As soon as the flagstaff went down, Beauregard, on Morris Island, started discussions with his men on how best to approach Anderson; he was sure the garrison was about to be burned alive. Meanwhile, on Cummings Point, the familiar manipulator, Louis T. Wigfall, now a member of Beauregard's staff, and made impetuous by a night of drinking, decided to try and claim for himself the glory of Anderson's surrender. Without permission, he went down to the creek, where he found a skiff, and with Private Gourdin Young of the Palmetto Guard, who carried a white flag, and two Negro oarsmen, pushed off into the harbor for Fort Sumter, while shells flew all around.

Colonel Ripley at Fort Moultrie saw the unidentified skiff and fired a warning shot across her bow but failed to frighten or slow up the Texas senator wearing the uniform of a colonel, so intent on capturing his prey.

Wigfall and his crew reached the Sumter landing safely and, finding the entrance to the fort on fire, crawled on all fours around the ripraps to the left face. Anderson, by this time informed of the curious and undignified party approaching him, sent Lieutenant Snyder and a soldier to investigate. Wigfall and Snyder met up at an embrasure on the left flank and Wigfall, waving in the lieutenant's face a sword with a white handkerchief fastened to its point, demanded to see Major Anderson. Three more Federal officers—Meade, Davis and Foster—confronted Wigfall inside the embrasure.

Then Major Robert Anderson appeared. "To what," he demanded, "am I indebted for this visit?"

"I am Colonel Wigfall, of General Beauregard's staff. For God's sake, Major, let this thing stop! There has been enough bloodshed already."

"There has been none on my side, and besides your batteries are still firing on me," Anderson said coldly, growing aware of Wigfall's unsteady condition.

Wigfall was determined. "I'll soon stop that," he said and turned to the Federal soldier, who now held the sword with the white handkerchief. "Wave that out there," he said officiously, and pointed toward the Confederate batteries. "Wave it yourself!" the soldier said and handed the sword back to Wigfall.

Wigfall accepted the challenge and was about to step through the embrasure when Anderson called out some advice: "If you want it to be seen you had better send it to the parapet." Wigfall walked unsteadily toward the parapet. The comedy continued as a shell burst very near by, stunning Wigfall out of his cavalier courage. "I have been fired upon with that flag two or three times," he shouted to Lieutenant Davis, who was the nearest man to him. "I think you might stand it once."

Wigfall retreated and seemed to come to his senses. Drawing himself up stiffly, he asked Anderson on what terms the major would evacuate the fort.

Anderson answered, "General Beauregard is already acquainted with my only terms."

"Do I understand," the South Carolina colonel pressed, "that you will evacuate upon the terms proposed the other day?"

"Yes, on those conditions only." Anderson stood his ground and would say no more to Wigfall, who muttered, "Very well," and took leave of the fort.

Anderson did not learn until later that Wigfall had been "AWOL" from Morris Island headquarters for two days; the ex-senator from Texas preferred to fight the war by himself.

Shortly after Wigfall's departure, Anderson took the inevitable, drastic step: he had the Stars and Stripes lowered and a white flag raised in its place. The steamer *Pocahontas,* delayed by the storm, had joined the fleet around two o'clock, her commander determined to shoot his way in at any cost. But before the ship could begin her run, the first and only real attempt to support Anderson with naval force, the surrender flag appeared over Sumter. The firing on both sides stopped.

General Beauregard, ignorant of Wigfall's visit to Sumter, saw the white flag go up. Anxious to prevent the fire that was clearly visible from destroying the entire fort, he instructed three of his aides to go to Sumter and find out if Anderson needed assistance; they were not to bother, for the moment, with working out the surrender terms. The three men—Captain Stephen Lee, William Porcher Miles, and Roger Pryor —boarded a small boat.

After being helped through an embrasure, they were conducted by Major Anderson to the hospital room which had been reinforced from floor to ceiling with boxes of sand. Surgeon Crawford's bed, table and medicine cabinet were still there among the bomb-

proofing. His officers formed a circle behind Anderson
as he seated himself across the table from the three
Southerners and heard them explain their mission.

Anderson heard them out. "Present my compliments to General Beauregard, and say to him that I
thank him for his kindness but need no assistance."
He explained to them that although the flames were
still active he had every expectation that the fire would
soon be under control. Suddenly he stopped, and then,
puzzled, he asked, "Gentlemen, do I understand you
come direct from General Beauregard?" The three
Southerners nodded.

"Why, Colonel Wigfall has just been here, by authority of General Beauregard, and proposed the same
terms of evacuation offered me on the 11th," Anderson told them angrily. They could only answer that
they had come direct from Beauregard and that, in
fact, Wigfall had not seen his general for several
days.

Convinced that he had been the victim of some sort
of hoax, Anderson threatened to run up the flag and
open fire again. But one of the aides convinced him
not to do so until they had communicated directly to
Beauregard the terms on which Anderson would consent to surrender.

While the deputation was waiting for Anderson to
write out his terms—essentially the same as he had
given Colonel Chesnut the day before—Roger Pryor
spied on the table before him a glass of liquid that he
assumed to be brandy. Bristling with Bowie knives
and pistols, armed as if he expected to make a singlehanded capture of the fort, Pryor boldly raised the
glass to his lips and drank. It was potassium iodide,
part of Crawford's medicinal kit. "Sir, you are a

dead man," Crawford said to Pryor, and the one-man attack force lapsed into terror. Despite the inclination of some of the Union officers to let the potassium iodide take its course, Crawford applied the stomach pump to Pryor and saved him.

At the conclusion of this grotesque episode, the three emissaries of Beauregard left to carry Anderson's terms to the general. They had come to Sumter with no orders to sue for terms; they had been pressed into diplomatic service by Anderson's threat to reopen the battle. Later that day two other emissaries arrived from Beauregard. Colonel Charles Allston, Jr. and Major David R. Jones were instructed to receive any propositions Anderson might wish to make.

Anderson met this new truce mission and read them a copy of the note he had earlier given Pryor, Miles and Lee. The new emissaries informed Anderson that since these were the same general terms he had given Chesnut, they would be acceptable. However, there was one condition that they could not now accept: Anderson's right to salute his flag as it was lowered— a point of honor. Pickens, rankled by his failure to reduce the fort by a spectacular and glorious military operation, had changed his mind about the salute and wished to impose a public humiliation on Anderson. The major, however, insisted on his point of honor and sent Allston and Jones back to Charleston with messages for both Beauregard and Pickens: he would stick to his surrender terms, including the ceremonial salute.

Pickens relented. At 7:00 P.M. an emissary presented Anderson with the final terms of surrender, as Anderson had insisted on them. The terms also specified that after he communicated with the Federal fleet and arranged for his evacuation, he was to agree that he was entirely responsible for the fort; otherwise Sumter would be garrisoned by four companies of Confederate artillery. Lieutenant Snyder was then sent off in a boat to arrange for a meeting with the fleet's commander.

Saturday night, April 13, was a dismal time for Sumter's men, who spent it packing their personal belongings, the hospital supplies and the remaining food, in preparation for abandoning their post the next morning.

That evening Charleston went wild with joy. Men on horseback galloped through the streets shouting the news. When the officers returned from Fort Sumter bearing the surrender agreement, they were followed by crowds, yelling and shouting with great enthusiasm. Mrs. Chesnut recalled: "I did not know that one could live through such days of excitement. Someone called: 'Come out! There is a crowd coming!' A mob it was, indeed, but it was headed by Colonels Chesnut and Manning. The crowd was shouting and showing these two as messengers of good news. They were escorted to Beauregard's headquarters. Fort Sumter had surrendered!"

When the hysterical populace reached the Charleston Hotel, Governor Pickens appeared on the balcony and addressed the crowd below, who cheered every time the Governor paused for breath. Pickens apologized for what would probably be a poor speech under the conditions. "In this open air, in such a noisy place, with the passing of vehicles"—but it was a masterpiece of lengthy bombast:

Thank God the day has come—thank God the war is open, and we will conquer or perish. They have vauntingly arrayed their twenty millions of men against us; they have exultingly, also, arrayed their navy, and they have called us but a handful of men, a weak and isolated state full of pride, and what they call chivalry, and with the hated institution of slavery, as they supposed a source of weakness, too, but which, in fact, is a source of strength in war; and they have defied us. But we have rallied; we have met them in the issues they have tendered in their stronghold, by which they expected to subjugate our country. We have met them and we have conquered. We have defeated their twenty millions, and we have made the proud flag of the Stars and Stripes, that never was lowered before to any nation on this earth—we have lowered it in humility before the Palmetto and the Confederate flags, and we have compelled them to raise by their side the white flag and ask for an honorable surrender. . . .

Pickens and the Charleston citizens he addressed were certain that the outcome of the thirty-four-hour bombardment of Sumter meant not only that Federal troops were driven from the harbor but that the war had already been won for the South. On this note of high confidence and jubilation, they celebrated the fall of Sumter.

CHAPTER
SIXTEEN

"With colors
flying and
drums beating"

It was all over but the withdrawal. Sunday, April 14,
dawned black for Anderson, brilliant for Beauregard.
After submitting to nearly four thousand shells, Sumter was hardly more than walls with a hole in the
center. The strong smell of smoldering wood rose in
the air and was carried by a stiff landward breeze
over the three and a third miles of harbor to the city
of Charleston, where her people sniffed it with de-
light and pride. The officers' quarters and barracks
were gutted by fire; the large studded main gate was a
pile of still-live ashes. The once-trim parade ground
was covered with mounds of sand and pitted with shell
holes, now pools of rainwater, reflecting the dazzling
April sky.

The outer walls remained upright but were permanently scarred with jagged holes left by shells;
along the parapet other shells had smashed the ma-

sonry, leaving great gaps. Among the wreckage of guns there, three were intact, one of them flying the improvised flagstaff with the Stars and Stripes snapping smartly from it.

The soldiers' dismal mood had not yet been sharpened by the touch of tragedy. For—incredible, miraculous, even ludicrous—in the thirty-four hours of bombardment not one solitary human being on either side had been killed or wounded, neither soldier, officer, spectator, man, woman or child. The impossible romance of battle had never been so explicitly realized. The dead consisted of one Confederate horse, which, tethered behind Fort Moultrie during the shooting, had been struck by a shell splinter and succumbed.

Fort Sumter became an object of curiosity and joy. Boats of all description sailed around and around her charred walls, like happy children. Fortunately for Anderson's dignity, none but official parties was permitted to land.

In Charleston people still stood at their observation places on wharves, docks, rooftops, and exulted. A correspondent reported, "On no gala occasion have we ever seen so large a number of ladies on our Battery as graced the breezy walk on this eventful morning."

However, a strong sentiment of chivalry filled these people, who expressed it in indignation that the Federal fleet had not come to Anderson's aid; it rather spoiled the symmetry of battle and, what is worse, seemed cowardly.

At 9:00 A.M. a steamer from Charleston, the *Isabel,* tied up at Sumter's wharf; it had come to take Anderson and his men away. A short time later, Lieutenant Snyder, who had been conferring with the Federal fleet outside the harbor, returned to the fort with several members of Beauregard's staff and Captain Gillis, commander of the *Pocahontas*. Preparations for evacuation went ahead without a hitch.

The salute to the United States flag was set for noon. A quietness had settled over the men at last released from tension and strain. They talked very little as they searched among the debris of the casemates for cartridges for the salute. Although fires were smoldering in the magazine, no one seemed to regard them as dangerous; it was not until days later that they finally expired.

Just before twelve o'clock the garrison formed in full uniform on the parade, their muskets, sidearms and other military accouterments glinting in the sunlight. Anderson instructed Privates Hough, Galloway and Fielding to mount to the parapet with two officers and take their stations at the salute gun. At the order to load they rammed a cartridge down the gun barrel. Anderson's loyal Mexican War sergeant, Peter Hart, stood at the flagstaff, ready to lower the flag. The breeze coming off the sea flew directly into the gun muzzle.

At the stroke of noon, a flash and a roar signaled the first of a proposed one hundred salutes, each a full charge of powder but no shot. There was an interval of a full minute between each salute; it took that long to reload and fire. Sergeant Hart was slowly lowering the flag.

At about 12:30 Governor Francis Pickens with his aides—General Jamison, General Hardee, Judge Magrath—and General Beauregard with his aides—Colonels Miles, Pryor, Manning, Chesnut, and Major Jones—boarded a steamer at Southern Wharf,

Charleston, and started out for Sumter and ceremonies of their own which were scheduled to take place there later in the day. Drawing near Sumter, they saw the empty *Isabel* and heard the gun salute still in progress; to avoid embarrassing Anderson by interrupting the ceremony, they turned and headed for Sullivan's Island to wait until it was over. There a carnival spirit prevailed. Officers and gentry enjoyed champagne and claret and French pâtés. Soldiers lounged in the dust and sunlight outside their tents, which bore inscriptions such as "Rattlesnake's Hole," "Yankee Smashers," "The Live Tigers." The war had begun for the South as an exciting and glorious adventure.

The Confederates were counting the salutes: forty-eight, forty-nine, fifty. At the fiftieth they heard something different, like two reports; they figured it was two guns being fired together. But they were wrong; it was something infinitely less expected. As Privates Hough, Galloway and Fielding were loading the gun for the fiftieth time, a fragment of cartridge bag was suddenly blown back by the wind, which carried it to the pile of powder at the rear of the gun. A tremendous explosion followed. Private Daniel Hough fell over dead, the first casualty of the Civil War. The right arm of Private Galloway was torn jaggedly from his shoulder; he died several days later. Private James Fielding was severely wounded. Here was the accident which brought war home to men's bosoms.

Surgeon Crawford came to the immediate aid of Galloway and Fielding. The body of Private Hough was covered and carried down from the parapet to the parade to await burial. The proposed 100-gun salute halted at an even fifty.

When Governor Pickens and General Beauregard heard the last double boom of Sumter's gun, they left Sullivan's Island where they had been waiting, reboarded their steamer and sailed out into the channel only to be met by a small boat whose lone occupant told them that one of Anderson's caissons had exploded and that fire-fighting equipment would certainly be needed. Once more Pickens' boat turned and made for Sullivan's Island, from which three fire companies of three men each, one engine and several hand pumps were dispatched by barge to aid Sumter.

It was now between two and three in the afternoon. The garrison was gloomily preparing for Hough's funeral, scheduled for four o'clock. In the meantime two additional fire companies had been ordered, along with a company of Beauregard's Regulars, to Sumter, as further precaution. The timing of their arrival, though unplanned, coincided with the funeral service. The Confederate soldiers, marching into the fort just as it was about to begin, formed ranks and uncovered while their own chaplain took over the reading.

When it was all over, Federal drummers beat out the unmistakable rhythm of "Yankee Doodle," and Anderson, the dignified, 56-year-old warrior, humiliated for the first time in his career, marched out of Sumter, his garrison behind him, and boarded the *Isabel*. As she sailed down the channel toward open sea, the Confederate troops lined the parapets of Sumter and cheered wildly, firing off all their guns in tribute to the men who had held out for so long.

The great gutted fort was now in Southern hands. The Stars and Bars and Palmetto flags flew side by side on the ramparts. Pickens and Beauregard had carried it off. The next step was up to President Lincoln.

On Monday morning, April 15, the same morning the President issued a call for 75,000 volunteers, Anderson and his men transferred from the *Isabel* to the *Baltic,* which headed north immediately. As the ship made for the open water and the route home, the men of Sumter lined her rails and gazed back over the stern. They did not go below until Charleston Harbor and its constellation of islands and forts were out of sight.

For most of the three-day journey to New York, Major Robert Anderson stayed in his cabin. He had maintained courage and dignity to the end; now that it was all over, now that he had been defeated, his strength failed, his spirit gave itself over to gloomy meditation. Safely aboard ship with him were the tattered, scarred flag of Sumter and the splintered staff from which it had last flown; Anderson intended that his body be lowered into the grave with the flag his shroud.

When the *Baltic* was off Sandy Hook, a few minutes out of New York, at 10:30 on the morning of April 18, Major Anderson composed his first and only report of the attack and his action. His hand so weak that he could not hold the pen steady, he dictated it to Captain Fox. It was short, clean, and objective:

> Having defended Fort Sumter for thirty-four hours, until the quarters were entirely burned, the main gates destroyed by fire, the gorge walls seriously impaired, the magazines surrounded by flames, and its door closed from the effects of the

heat, four barrels and three cartridges of powder only being available, and no provisions remaining but pork, I accepted terms of evacuation offered by General Beauregard (being the same offered by him on the 11th instant, prior to the commencement of hostilities), and marched out of the fort on Sunday afternoon, the 14th instant, with colors flying and drums beating, bringing away company and private property, and saluting my flag with fifty guns.

ROBERT ANDERSON
Major, First Artillery

HONORABLE SIMON CAMERON
Secretary of War
Washington, D.C.

And the Federal ships sent to bring him arms, men and provisions, the occasion of the battle in Charleston Harbor and of months of diplomatic negotiations and military planning—the entire expedition had been a dismal failure, conceived in haste and executed too late. Captain Gustavus Fox, the planner and commander of the expedition, who had been certain that his ships could reach Sumter with little risk, could claim with some justice that the blame was not all his. The *Powhatan* had never arrived (although the ship was probably of too deep a draft to cross the harbor bar, she did carry necessary launches). Nor had the two tugs, *Uncle Ben* and *Yankee,* on which Fox depended for his actual landing, ever arrived either. The northeast gale had driven the *Uncle Ben* into the arms of the Secessionists at Wilmington, North Carolina; the *Yankee,* forced into Savannah Harbor by the storm, escaped capture by the South but arrived off Charleston only after Anderson had been evacuated. The *Baltic* had come close to disaster on Rattlesnake Shoals, and the entire expedition had been menaced by storm and heavy seas. The *Pawnee* and *Harriet Lane* were both short of men and, according to Fox, had been intended only as bases of operations while the tugs fought their way in. The *Pocahontas,* which might have made the run to Sumter, had arrived too late. Like so many of the other plans and projects, big and little, that led up to the firing on Fort Sumter, Fox's expedition was riddled by hesitations and counterorders, intrigue and miscalculation, the vagaries of nature, and pure bad luck.

Gales and guns notwithstanding, one ship did enter the harbor on the night of April 12. It was a sloop carrying a load of wood for a Charleston resident, and it was piloted by an old Negro. He had been warned that it would be dangerous to attempt to land, that he would probably be killed on the way. The determination of his reply, as reported by a Charleston newspaper—"Caint hep that. Must go to de town tonight: if anybody hurt dis boat, Massa see him about it, shuah!"—must have helped carry him in safely and seemed a rebuke to the mighty Union fleet.

Lincoln felt that he owed Fox an apology for the failure of the expedition. On May 1 he wrote:

> I sincerely regret that the failure of the late attempt to provision Fort Sumter should be the source of annoyance to you. The practicability of your plan was not, in fact, brought to the test. By reason of a gale, well known in advance to be possible and not improbable, the tugs, an essential part of the plan, never reached the ground, while by an accident, for which you were in no wise re-

sponsible, and possibly I to some extent was, you were deprived of a war vessel with her men, which you deemed of great importance to the enterprise. I most cheerfully and truly declare that the failure of the expedition has not lowered you a particle, while the qualities you developed in the effort have greatly heightened you in my estimation. For a daring and dangerous enterprise of a similar character you would today be the man of all my acquaintances whom I would select.

The *Baltic* docked at New York City on April 18. A large, enthusiastic crowd was at the dock to meet the men and give them a heroes' welcome. The New York *Herald* reported that the demonstrations for Anderson had been "seldom exceeded by the generous heart of New York."

Two young ladies of New York, Abby and Jane Woolsey—whose cousin, William Aspinwall, had for the past days spent hours trying to console the distraught Mrs. Robert Anderson—were caught up in the general excitement that greeted the first hero of the Civil War. Like the nice, articulate, observant creatures that they were, they recorded their firsthand reactions in journals. Abby wrote:

We clung to an iron railing inside an adjoining courtyard and, safe from the crush of the crowd, waved our welcome with the rest and saw Major Anderson come out, bow with military precision several times, and then retire. He looked small, slender, old, wrinkled, and grey, and was subdued and solemn in manner.

Her sister looked and also listened:

Major Anderson is very grave, almost sad, in expression and manner, as a man may well be who has been through such scenes and looks with a wise eye into such a future; but if anything could cheer a man's soul it would be such enthusiasm and almost love as are lavished on him here. He says they had not had a biscuit to divide among them for nearly two days, and were almost suffocated. They say he talks very little about it all; only gives facts in a few modest words. He is "overwhelmed" with the sight of the enthusiasm and unanimity of the North; "the South has no idea of it at all." He says that he "felt very much aggrieved at being attacked with such disadvantage"; that for four weeks he only received *one* message from the Government, and was almost broken down with suspense, anxiety, and ignorance of what was required of him. . . . He goes about with tears in his eyes all the time.

The New York Chamber of Commerce publicly presented Anderson with the Sumter Medal, which displayed a portrait of him on one side and on the reverse bore the verbose legend "The Genius or Guardian Spirit of America arising from Fort Sumter" and the inscription "The Chamber of Commerce, New York, honors the defender of Fort Sumter—the patriot, the hero, the man." He was commercialized as well: novelty portraits of Anderson were advertised in all publishers' windows and in the newspapers, and D. Appleton & Company, of 445 Broadway, advertised "A Fine Engraving of Major Anderson, 15 ×17, Price 25¢—and on India paper, $1.00—also Cartes des Visites 25¢."

So many people crowded Union Square on April 20 to honor and catch a glimpse of the heroic defender of Sumter that he was forced to present himself at each of five grandstands. He smiled, nodded, and waved to the crowds, but did not make a speech. The New York *Herald* reporter, carried away by enthusiasm, wrote this story of the ceremonies: "Such a mighty uprising of the people has never before been witnessed in New York, nor throughout the whole length and breadth of the Union." During the afternoon the flag of Sumter, still fastened to the improvised staff, half shot away, was placed incongruously in the hand of the equestrian statue of General Washington.

On the same day President Lincoln asked Simon Cameron to write a letter to Anderson and his men, thanking him and sanctioning his inevitable retreat. "I am directed by the President of the United States," the message read, "to communicate to you, and through you, to the officers and men under your command, at Forts Moultrie and Sumter, the approbation of the Government of your and their judicious and gallant conduct there, and to tender to you and them the thanks of the Government for the same."

Ten days later Lincoln himself wrote Anderson "a purely private and social letter, to say I shall be much gratified to see you here at your earliest convenience, when and where I can, perhaps explain some things on my part, which you may not have understood." On this cryptic note the drama of Fort Sumter came to a close. Did Lincoln intend to explain the failure of the Fox expedition, the doubts he may have had of Anderson's loyalty and competence, his slowness in taking action, a policy of provoking or at least permitting the Southern side to initiate the first action of the war? We will never know.

Lincoln had lost Sumter but had gained a united North. This almost bloodless first engagement, the focal point of ambiguities and hesitations, cross-purposes and the delusions of chivalry, signaled the start of a war which, when it came to an end four years later, had cost the lives of nearly a million men on both sides and changed the face and conscience of the nation.

EPILOGUE | "The loyal
reticence
of the man"

The Confederates had taken Fort Sumter. By a log-
ical transition, from "Bastion of the Union" Sumter now became the "Citadel of Rebellion," maintaining her strategic usefulness, her symbolic efficacy.
The South rejoiced, although it was fast discovering
that Sumter's capture was not an end to the struggle
but a beginning. Throughout the war the fort was considered by both sides as a desirable prize, the key to
the city of Charleston, a man-made edifice of tran-
scendent appeal standing for ultimate goals.

In 1862 Sumter was rebuilt and rearmed by the
Confederates to withstand a series of Federal assaults
by sea and by land. Determined to complete the Federal blockade of Southern ports and seal off Charleston by taking Sumter, a fleet of Northern ironclads
commanded by Admiral Samuel F. Du Pont tried, in
April 1863, to enter the harbor but withdrew after

suffering heavy damage. Later that year three thousand Northern infantrymen, commanded by Anderson's
former subordinate, Truman Seymour, now a brigadier general, stormed over Morris Island, but even
with the support of massive artillery trained on Sumter they could not take it. Continual bombardment
from shore installations and war vessels failed to reduce Sumter, which only grew stronger as her walls
crumbled into impenetrable mounds of rubble. Her garrison of 300 men, secure behind these mounds and
behind sandbags and wooden pikes, held out until February 1865. It was not bombardment or landing attempts that finally caused her commander to surrender, but the arrival of General Sherman's forces in
the state capital of Columbia on their march to the
sea. Charleston surrendered bloodlessly to a Negro
regiment from Massachusetts, and on February 18,
1865, after nearly four years, the United States flag
flew over Sumter again. Countless shells had fallen on
the fort and had been fired from her. When Sumter
was opened as a national monument in 1948, some
of these shells, buried in the ground, were still live
and had to be detonated, a last echo of the conflict.

Although, in the celebrations that followed the retaking of Sumter, Anderson came out of retirement to
be hailed once more as its hero, he remained an enigma.
To his contemporaries, even to those who had served
with him, his conduct in all his days at Moultrie and
Sumter was not so clear-cut as they would have
wished it to be. Some questioned his loyalty, others the
wisdom of his military decisions. Some saw him as a
mere pawn of Lincoln's, his function to draw the fire
of the Confederates and his duty to kill no one. And
while most of the Northern newspapers saw the bat-

tle for Sumter in a heroic light, others took a more cynical view. "The administration had no intention of making a fight at Sumter," the Pittsburgh *Gazette* declared soon after Anderson's surrender; the siege of Fort Sumter was "perhaps the broadest farce in the annals of warfare, and one that will elicit shouts of laughter throughout the world."

It is an irony, perhaps, that Anderson should have been the man at the center of the drama. He reflected, in microcosm, the scruples and conflicts of the entire country—the lack of policy, the divisions and inconsistencies that had both scattered and marshaled the forces of war. He was a man of good intentions, humane, religious, peace-loving. He was pro-Union but also pro-slavery. He believed in the Southern cause, but he balked at the way in which it was being advanced. Above all, he did not want to be the cause of war. Like the Federal Government during the immediate prewar months, Anderson's behavior was contradictory and ambiguous, and, like the Union, he suffered for it.

Anderson's daughter, Eba Lawton, wrote a book in which she attempted to defend her father against charges of disloyalty and incompetence which were brought against him almost from the day he moved from Moultrie to Sumter. Eba summed up one aspect of the Sumter affair: "The public orders were to defend the fort to the last extremity. The secret 'confidential' order instructed the major to give up the fort without a fight. It is an evidence of the loyal reticence of the man that he kept this secret to himself throughout his life." Even though Eba was in error about how long Anderson kept Secretary of War Floyd's infamous order from his officers, her point is clear: whatever his personal conflict, Anderson had been offered a choice of loyalties, and he rejected Floyd. Anderson's motivations (and his hesitancies) Eba related to a statement of the major's which rings true, even though it appears to have been poetically embellished: "Our Southern brethren have done grievously wrong. They have rebelled and have attacked their father's house and their loyal brothers. They must be punished, but this necessity breaks my heart."

Captain Abner Doubleday, later raised to major general, was a literate and analytical soldier who also wrote an account of Sumter and her commander. This is what he said in Anderson's defense: "Major Anderson was neither timid nor irresolute, and he was fully aware of his duties and responsibilities. Unfortunately he desired not only to save the Union but to save slavery with it. He could not read the signs of the times and see that the conscience of the nation and the progress of civilization had already doomed slavery to destruction." This is undoubtedly nearer the truth than an admiring daughter is likely to approach. It explains Anderson's reluctance to take the offensive, his overfriendliness with Southern officers and emissaries, perhaps even his excessive caution.

Had Anderson faced a foreign enemy his duty would have been clearly defined. But his position in Fort Sumter was unique, and the pressures on him both to act and to refrain from acting were tremendous. The man was not of heroic stature or decisiveness, but he did his best to follow his own convictions so long as they accorded with loyalty to the Union. His enemies included an impetuous and crafty Southerner, Pickens, who tried to harry him into firing the first shot, and a treacherous chief, Floyd, who attempted to use Anderson's dilemma for his own purposes. His supporters included an indecisive president, Buchanan, who wished above all to retire from office before the outbreak of war, and Lincoln, whose newness to the politics and forces at work and doubts of Anderson himself caused him to delay the psychological and military backing the major needed so desperately. When Lincoln did act, he was too late and he planned inadequately. Caught in such circumstances, a bolder man than Anderson might have succeeded only in starting the war a month or two earlier.

Anderson's main concern had been to prevent conflict or, as it appeared inevitable, to postpone it as long as possible. Of his move from Moultrie to Sumter, he wrote to his Charleston friend, Robert Gourdin: "Not one person of my command knew of my determination until that morning, and only on that day. I did it because in my opinion it was the best way of preventing the shedding of blood." And in another letter to Gourdin: "I am now, thank God, in a place which will, by His helping hand, soon be made so strong that the South Carolinians will be madmen if they attack me!"

Anderson's move to Sumter had seemed to put him out of the reach of the Secessionists, even though in a short while he began to feel like the sheep about to be slaughtered. This move of great boldness and decisiveness, a move for which Anderson was prepared to accept abuse from both North and South (and for which he received a Congressional vote of confidence), had been motivated by defensive and pacifist considerations. As time went on, and as the tensions both mounted and narrowed in focus, these motives had been more and more tempered by a caution which Anderson's critics interpreted as passive, or permissive, disloyalty to the Union cause. Despite Southern threats, sanctions, diplomatic and psychological offensives, he refused to be forced into firing the first shot. If, in retrospect, his diplomatic dealings with Pickens' envoys seem lacking in self-reliance, they did succeed in holding off the catastrophe and carrying out what passed for a Federal policy of non-provocation.

A man more impulsive and aggressive, less sensitive to the meanings of the act, might have come to the defense of the *Star of the West*. But Anderson had felt that his hands were tied by his orders from Washington and by the fact that he had not been told to support the expedition. He could have taken the initiative, closed the harbor, and forced a state of war. Instead he had sent an officer to Washington. In the eyes of *The New York Times*, "Major Anderson yielded to the menaces of Governor Pickens and consented to await further instructions from Washington. The result of all this"—with the implication that Anderson had intended it so—"is that the disunionists have ample leisure to complete their preparations. It is useless to deny that the conduct of Major Anderson stands in need of some explanation." Yet Anderson was observing Federal policy, indecisive, contradictory and procrastinating as that was. His critics ignored the fact that his duty and loyalty to the Union had to consist in following "policy," and not making it.

Another question mark rests uncomfortably on Anderson's apparently conflicting reports of January and February. In the first he had declared that "I do not consider it good policy to send reinforcements here at this time. We can hold out as long as it is necessary to do so." In the second, which reached Lincoln's desk a day after the Inauguration, he had made an urgent demand for reinforcements—twenty thousand men with armed naval escort. This was the report which had sent Lincoln to Secretary of War Holt with serious questioning of Anderson's loyalty and reliability. At the end of March Lincoln had had to deny the request of a Congressional committee to release Anderson's dispatches; it was a matter of security, the President said. And at the same time some of the nation's newspapers, among them *The New York Times,* were reporting that in the upper echelons of the Government there were grave doubts about Anderson's motives.

Why had Anderson, within the space of a month and a half, changed his tone and his terms so radically? There is a hint of an answer in his reply to a Rhode Island lady who wrote to ask him why the Government had not sent him reinforcements: "I knew that the moment it should be known that additional troops were coming, the South Carolinians would assault me and thus inaugurate civil war. My policy, secure for the present in my stronghold, was to keep still, preserve the peace, to give time for the quieting of the excitement, in the hope of avoiding bloodshed." His first consideration had clearly been to avert an open conflict. In writing his first dispatch he had used it to rationalize himself into a tenable position and an unrealistic bravado: "We can hold out as long as it is necessary to do so."

As tension mounted, as food supplies dwindled, as his men grew weak and morale sagged, he had been forced to recognize that the situation was frightful, that postponing conflict was not going to solve his problem, that without help it was now a question of surrendering or starving. And the fact that even by the end of February the Government had not formulated a definite policy for Sumter tormented him in his isolation and made him less capable of evaluating his position and the effect that his second dispatch would have in Washington.

As to Anderson's surrender of the fort, Senator Charles Sumner of Massachusetts wrote: "The conduct of Major Anderson, though generally applauded at the time, has not escaped criticism, and the wisdom, if not the patriotism of this act, has been called into question." The questioning came from, among others, Anderson's own engineer officer, Captain Foster, and also from two of Beauregard's aides who had had direct dealings with Anderson, Colonel Chisholm and Captain Hartstene.

The latter two were convinced that Anderson could have held out longer. "I have always been of the opinion that Major Anderson should not have surrendered when he did," Chisholm wrote. "The walls were secure, and he still had provisions which would have sustained his small command until the fleet could both provision and reinforce him. I was present with Captain Hartstene during the evacuation and was astonished to see barrels of pork being rolled out and shipped aboard the *Isabel*." And Hartstene added: "One bold officer in command of a navy barge armed with a boat howitzer could have easily cleared the way for a hundred barges with men and supplies to pass the fort."

And from Captain Foster: "We could have resumed the firing as soon as the walls cooled sufficiently to open the magazines; and then, having blown down the wall left projecting above the parapet, so as to get rid of flying bricks, and built up the main gate with stones and rubbish, the fort would actually have been in a more defensible condition than when the action commenced."

What all three critics seem to miss, however valid their military logic, is that there would have been no point in the major's holding out longer than he did. Yes, he did have provisions, but they were all in the form of preserved pork, hardly nourishment for fighting men who had not tasted green vegetables or fresh meat in weeks. Yes, the fleet might have been able to run the gauntlet of Southern batteries—but it did not, and after more than thirty hours of bombardment Anderson was fairly sure (though unable to say why) that it would not attempt to reach the fort. And, finally, what could have been acomplished by his holding out longer than he did? The opening guns of the Civil War had been fired; the war he so dreaded was now an actuality; his role as a holdout was over. As long as the Federal ships stood idly at the harbor entrance, there was nothing for Anderson to do but surrender. The sooner he did so the less likely it was that one of his own men would be killed. It may have been Seward, with his last-minute decision to detach the *Powhatan* with its indispensable landing barges, who settled Sumter's fate and thereby caused doubt to focus on Anderson.

Anderson remained silent to the attacks upon him. By December 1862 his illness, diagnosed by Army physicians as "softening of the brain"—a deterioration of the brain centers, not unrelated to paresis— had progressed so far that he was forbidden by his doctors to engage in correspondence. Even so he dictated a letter to Secretary of War Stanton to protest the promotion of Captain Foster, his critic and an officer with whom he had clearly had disagreements. He was generous in his praise of Doubleday and Crawford and implored Stanton "that the distinction now contemplated for only one of the officers shall not be bestowed alone, it being in my estimation neither deserved upon his part nor just to his brother officers." He promised "an official report of the closing scenes of the occupancy of Sumter, which I have thus far been prevented from complying with by the strict orders of my physician."

In 1869, four years after Lee's surrender and after he had briefly emerged from private life to appear at the flag-raising ceremonies at Sumter, Anderson left for Europe with his wife, hoping to find abroad a cure or some relief for his disease. This was the trip he had once planned when war seemed imminent and he still thought it possible that he could be an observer only, and not an actor. Now it was nearly too late. The Andersons went to the French Midi, where they lived for two years. On October 27, 1871, in Nice, Major General Anderson died. His body was brought back in the man-of-war *Guerrière* for funeral services at Fortress Monroe in Virginia and in New York City. He was buried at West Point, where his career as a soldier had begun. Heartsick at the conflict between North and South, exhausted by his ordeal at Sumter, he had been, in a sense, the first casualty of the war he never wanted to fight.

ACKNOWLEDGMENTS AND BIBLIOGRAPHY

It would not have been possible to write this book in its present form and in the time allotted if it had not been for two friends of mine, Justin and Anne Kaplan, who gave patiently of their time and expert editorial assistance in the preparation of the manuscript through a very trying and busy period. They have my grateful appreciation and thanks.

I am indebted also to Miss Shirley Spranger of the American History staff of the New York Public Library for her unfailing courtesy and help in locating old but important books indispensable to the story; and to Milton Kaplan and Virginia Daiker of the Library of Congress, who have never failed to come to my assistance when I needed it; and to Fran Stager, who typed the research notes and papers. Finally, for many reasons beyond research assistance, I am indebted to Anne Meredith.

The following is a list of books and other source materials consulted for *Storm Over Sumter:*

Anderson, Major Robert. *An Artillery Officer in the Mexican War.* New York, 1911.

Anderson, Major Robert. *The True Stories of Pickens and Sumter* and *Political Conspiracies Preceding the Rebellion.* New York, 1882.

Beauregard, General P. G. T. *The Defense of Charleston* in *Battles and Leaders of the Civil War.* New York, 1884.

Buchanan, James. *Buchanan's Administration.* New York, 1866.

Callahan, G. A. *Diplomatic History of the Southern Confederacy.* Baltimore, 1901.

Chesnut, Mary Boykin. *A Diary From Dixie.* New York, 1905.

Chester, Captain James. *Inside Sumter in '61* in *Battles and Leaders of the Civil War.* New York, 1884.

Crawford, Major General S. W. *Genesis of the Civil War.* New York, 1887.

Curry, J. L. M. *Civil History of the Government of the Confederate States.* Richmond, 1901.

Davis, Jefferson. *The Rise and Fall of the Confederate Government.* New York, 1876.

Doubleday, Major General Abner. *Reminiscences of Fort Sumter and Fort Moultrie.* New York, 1876.

Fox, Gustavus Vasa. *Report on the Relief Expedition to Fort Sumter. Official Records of the War of the Rebellion.*

Freemantle, Arthur Lyon. *Three Months in the Southern States.* London, 1863.

Harris, W. A. *The Record of Fort Sumter from Its Occupation by Major Anderson to Its Reduction by Confederate Troops.* Columbia, South Carolina, 1862.

Hayward, John. *A Gazetteer of the United States of America.* Philadelphia, 1854.

Lawton, Eba Anderson. *Robert Anderson and Fort Sumter.* New York, 1911.

Lee, Captain Stephen D. *The First Step in the War* in *Battles and Leaders of the Civil War.* New York, 1884.

Moore, Frank. *Fort Sumter Memorial.* New York, 1869.

Nicolay, John G. *The Outbreak of the Rebellion.* New York, 1898.

Pollard, Edward A. *The Rival Administrations.* Richmond, 1863.

Pollard, Edward A. *Southern History of the War in the United States.* Toronto, Canada, 1863.

Roman, Alfred. *Life and Military Operations of General Beauregard.* New York, 1883.

Russell, William Howard. *My Diary North and South.* New York, 1954.

St. Mery, Moreau de. *American Journey.* Edited by Kenneth Roberts. New York, 1947.

Sandburg, Carl. *Abraham Lincoln: The War Years.* Vol. 1. New York, 1939.

JOURNALS

Journal of the Convention of the People of South Carolina. 1860.

The Battle of Fort Sumter and *First Victory of the Southern Troops.*

Detailed Reports of the Charleston Press. Charleston, 1861.

Major Anderson at Fort Sumter. Massachusetts Historical Society Papers. Boston, 1912. Vol. 9, pp. 1-52.

MONOGRAPHS

Glover, Gilbert G. *Immediate Pre-Civil War Compromise Efforts.* Nashville, 1909.

NEWSPAPERS

Buffalo *Daily Courier*
Charleston *Courier*
Charleston *Mercury*
Chicago *Tribune*
Cincinnati *Commercial*

Cleveland *Plain Dealer*
Augusta, Georgia, *Constitutionalist*
New York *Herald*
New York *Times*

STANDARD BIBLIOGRAPHY

War of the Rebellion (Official Records), Vol. 1, Series L., Washington, 1880.

CORRESPONDENCE

Letters of Major Robert Anderson. New York Public Library.

MISCELLANEOUS

The Confederate States Almanac, Richmond, 1861. (Weather Reports)

The Strangers Guide and Official Directory. Richmond, 1863.

New York City Directory. 1860-61. New York Public Library.

Narrative of General William Henry Trescot. (Quoted in *Genesis of the Civil War,* S. W. Crawford.)

PERIODICALS

The Index. A Weekly Journal of Politics, Literature and News. Vol. 1, Richmond, 1862.

INDEX

ABOUT THE AUTHOR

ROY MEREDITH's *illustrated biography of the great photographer Mathew B. Brady,* Mr. Lincoln's Camera Man, *was published in 1946 and is regarded as one of the key books in the current revival of interest in the Civil War period. Since then Mr. Meredith has published three other books:* The Face of Robert E. Lee, Mr. Lincoln's Contemporaries, *and an illustrated military history,* The American Wars.

A native New Yorker, Mr. Meredith attended Columbia University and the University of Pennsylvania. He has been a writer and director in both films and television and during World War II he served as a cinematographer with the Fifth AAF Combat Film Detachment.

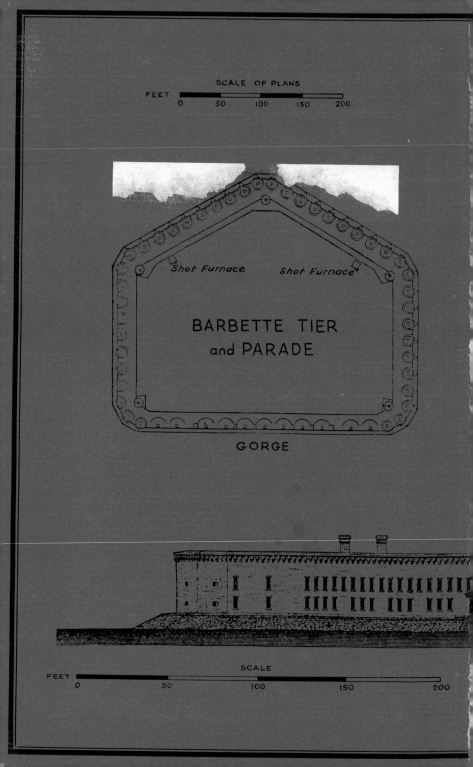

SCALE OF PLANS

FEET 0 50 100 150 200

Shot Furnace   Shot Furnace

BARBETTE TIER
and PARADE

GORGE

SCALE

FEET 0 50 100 150 200